INTRODUCTION

PART 1 – THE MAIN CAUSES OF MENTAL I

- Loss of Identitity; Guilt; Shame; Regret; Anger
Unforgiveness & Fear_____

PART 2 – THE NEGATIVE HABITS AND BEHAVIOURS THAT MENTAL BAGGAGE CAUSE.

DISCLAIMER

The information contained in this book is intended to help readers to support themselves to achieve their goals. The advice presented is general. Always consult a qualified practitioner for individual treatment. This book is not a substitute for counselling, and the reader should consult with their General Practitioner or qualified professional regarding any issues relating to their emotional or mental health.

The examples portrayed in this book are fictitious and are for illustrative purposes only. While they are reflective of typical client presentations, they are products of the author's imagination and any resemblance to actual persons is purely coincidental. However, my personal illustrations are all true.

ACKNOWLEDGEMENTS

To my wonderful husband, Raymond – You are not just my partner in life, but you're my best friend. Thank you for believing in me and always supporting me. I also want to give thanks to my family, who have been such a blessing with their supportive words. My daughter Nicola, son-in-law Brian, Son Jonathan, daughter-in-law Sandra; grandchildren, Callum; Lauren; Matthew; Alex; Sophie and Sam. Also my brother Albert, cousin Marjorie and God-daughter Eliza. Not forgetting my stepdaughter Charlotte, Lee and Rosie. Special thanks to my friends, Davy, Kathleen; Joanne, Brian, Frank and Tracie, for their support and prayers. Also, a thank you to my counselling supervisor Hilda who has kept me sane throughout the year.

Many thanks to Louise Dixen, who created a fantastic book cover, Brian Cross for his editorial expertise and Jasmine Munn for her amazing formatting skills.

INTRODUCTION

I felt drawn to write this book for several reasons. First and foremost, I think it will help many people understand themselves in a way they have never experienced before. I aim to highlight the impact emotional baggage has on everyday life. The main baggage culprits are: unforgiveness, anger, regret, guilt, fear, and loss of identity.

I have worked in Private Practice and the voluntary sector as a counsellor for many years. This role has allowed me to be in a privileged position of getting to know so many amazing people. It has also given me an insight of identifying a common thread that runs through most people's lives. The common thread I am talking about is how efficiently they deal with present and past trauma. e.g., unforgiveness, anger, regrets, etc. It's not so much the actual enormity of the injustice, but it's more how good they are at letting it go afterwards. By not processing these issues correctly, they are subconsciously stacking them up for an inevitable fall.

A lot of people mistakenly feel they have dealt with past trauma by burying it deep into their unconscious mind. Yes, they may feel they have sorted it out by making it disappear. However, by burying it, they have unfortunately buried it alive. That is why so many people struggle with traumas that have resurrected from their past. They end up feeling confused and lost and lose touch with who they are. The lesson to be learned is don't hold on to anything longer than you need to. In other words, 'Travel Light.'

Part one of the book outlines the major causes of mental baggage that we carry in our unconscious mind, such as guilt, shame, anger, fear, and unforgiveness. Just like physical baggage, mental baggage doesn't appear overnight. It's an accumulation of years of pain and unhealthy behaviours. Feelings of inadequacy and worthlessness are so common.

When a person comes from a neglected and abusive past, it can, unfortunately, be the catalyst for carrying negative, destructive emotions such as guilt, shame, anger, etc. Unfortunately, if these negative emotions are not processed correctly, the load gets heavier and eventually unbearable.

Part two of the book explains the unhealthy behaviours that people adopt to help facilitate these issues from their past. These behaviours, unfortunately, tend to turn out to be more of a problem than the original issue. It can range from angry outbursts, addictions, burnouts, people-pleasing, and the tendency of attracting toxic people into their lives.

'People pleasing' can have a detrimental effect on how the person views themselves. Unfortunately, by not valuing who they are, it then has a knock-on effect on their self-esteem and self-confidence.

This book highlights how important and precious you are as a person. It will also outline how important you are to God. People seem to think that being a Christian will take away stress and worry. Not so, as long as we are living in a fallen world, we too will be susceptible to negative emotions. However, if we have the Holy Spirit residing in our hearts, we will have a better chance of making healthier choices during those challenging times.

Culturally, sometimes we are taught, its selfish to see to our needs before others. However, we need to feel valuable and important to ourselves as well as to God. When we show kindness and love to ourselves, as God does, we find it then easier to project that love to others. Part two also explains why we become vulnerable, needy, and clingy in our relationships, and why we tend to be drawn to the same toxic people time after time.

Part three provides strategies and coping mechanisms on how to let go of the clutter and baggage in our head. It will show us techniques on how to deal with toxic people and to learn to become more assertive and to validate ourselves. It will also help us to heal from unhealthy relationships and help with setting up healthy boundaries.

This book will show that by letting go of unwanted mental baggage, it will make us feel lighter and give us more clarity on who we are. It will make a vast difference to our everyday life as we won't be weighed down by the shame, anger, and regrets that held us a prisoner for years

To sum up the introduction of this book, I will draw on the metaphor of a 'train' to demonstrate its similarity with our life's journey. When a train departs the station, it's at the start of a person's life. The accompanying people, at the beginning of the journey, are usually parents and siblings.

As the train travels from station to station, different experiences and traumas may take place. Unfortunately, this sometimes can be the root cause of carrying mental baggage. Sometimes the baggage may more than likely belong to a person from our past; in other words, it may have belonged to someone who got off the train miles back. When we realise it's not our baggage, we have to dump it immediately at the next station. In other words, keep 'Travelling light'.

PART 1

THE MAIN CAUSES OF MENTAL BAGGAGE

- Loss of Identitity; Guilt; Shame; Regret; Anger; Unforgiveness & Fear

CHAPTER 1

- THE HEAVY BURDEN OF NOT KNOWING WHO YOU ARE.

Have you ever felt lost and don't know who you are? So many people get to the stage in their life that they don't recognise the person they have become. Feeling angry and irritated is an everyday occurrence. You probably don't even like yourself anymore. It's so easy to fall into this trap of losing oneself. One day you're a busy working parent with a career. Your kids go to the best school. Your standard of living is what most people dream of. However, something is missing. It doesn't feel enough. Every day is a struggle to keep going. You always feel tired and disillusioned. You can't understand why you are discontent as you have everything you ever dreamed of.

Letting that go and starting to be less critical with oneself is a great start. However, it's not easy changing our habits and mindset. So what is wrong – why can't we relax and enjoy our life. For a start, it's all to do with what core beliefs we hold. Not only do core beliefs affect how we view the world, but they also affect how we see oneself.

CORE BELIEFS

Our Core Belief needs to be accurate and correct. If distorted, it can, unfortunately, harm how we live our lives.

So what is a Core Belief, what makes it so important? Well, for a start, its all about our beliefs and assumptions. It's the view you have of yourself as well as the view you have of the world.

Core Beliefs are not something we consciously think about; when we sit down and try to identify them, we can then start to understand the impact they have on us. Core Beliefs are important because they affect how we think, how we feel, and lastly how we act. They are based on early experiences when the mind was open to interpretations of other people. As time goes on, they somehow get buried in our subconscious.

The following are examples of negative core beliefs and the impact they can have on our life.

1. CORE BELIEF: The world is a dangerous place.
 IMPACT: I hate leaving my home in case something awful happens.

2. CORE BELIEF: I would like a boyfriend, but I know all men are disloyal and untrustworthy.
IMPACT: Lives a solitary and lonely life, too afraid to get hurt. The core belief makes all men unfaithful.

3. CORE BELIEF: If you try something new, and you don't succeed, everyone will laugh at you.
IMPACT: You will never branch out and try something different, as you will be too afraid.

4. CORE BELIEF: I feel unattractive and useless.
IMPACT: When someone compliments you, you never believe them.

5. CORE BELIEF: My mother told me I was a mistake; I was never meant to be born.
IMPACT: I'm not wanted. If I wasn't here, no one would ever miss me.

6. CORE BELIEF: It's selfish ever to have your own opinion or meet your individual needs.
IMPACT: I let people walk over me as I feel they are right. My needs are not essential.

7. CORE BELIEF: If I don't please and make everyone happy, I must be an awful person.
IMPACT: Always trying to fix things for other people but never glad yourself.

8. CORE BELIEF: I suffer from depression. Therefore I am not a proper Christian.
IMPACT: Don't feel a true Christian. Robbed of the joy of knowing the Lord.

Take, for instance, the first two Core Beliefs: The world is a dangerous place, and all men are untrustworthy. As you see, the impact of these Beliefs will leave a person not knowing who they are, and the chances are they will end up living a life that is reclusive and unsatisfying.

Therefore it important to either challenge or discard Core Beliefs, especially if they are stopping you from living the life you desire.

WHY DO I FEEL WORTHLESS

Have you ever looked in the mirror and thought, 'I look a mess, who on earth would ever love me.' Believe it or not, this is a common phrase that a lot of people would say to themselves. They feel they are worthless and put little value on who they are. Of course, there are times when we all dislike who we are; however, if we loathe our actions and thoughts continually, it can be a sure sign of low self-esteem issues. Our worst critic is ourselves. This internal critic repeatedly tells us that we are stupid and unlovable. Unfortunately, this voice is so convincing; we come to believe that what it says is true. We are so familiar with this voice as it's been a companion of ours for years. Unfortunately, this companion is not a true friend.

To silence this internal critic, we have to consciously challenge the negative voice in our head by replacing the lie with an alternative statement. It's not easy, but with practice and determination, the old critic voice will soon start to disappear. Try and be your own best friend. Remember, if you wouldn't say these harsh things to your best friend, why on earth would you say it to yourself.

HIGH ACHIEVERS - LOW SELF-ESTEEM ISSUES

High achievers are sometimes prone to low self-esteem issues, mainly because they live with a constant sense of failure. Their identity has always been tied up with having impressive results. Anything less than perfect is a failure to them. These unrealistic expectations can take their toll on your joy and well-being.

SELF-LOATHING

Self-loathing can happen when a person is brought up in a home where they experienced years of neglect from their caregivers. They felt worthless and of no value and taught that they didn't deserve love as they were useless. Unfortunately, the child would grow up believing these false statements. Similarly, if an adult has had a secure childhood and then encountered emotional abuse later in life, this, unfortunately, can then contribute to a distortion of their self-image beliefs. Significant events such as a divorce can also add to eroding the foundations of a person's self-worth.

LOW SELF-ESTEEM - INDECISION

People with low self-esteem are usually indecisive people. They find it hard to make a decision. It may take them a considerable time to ponder over a very simplistic decision. Their fear of getting it wrong has a significant impact on them; it usually leaves them in a position of 'sitting on the fence'.

You will find a person who has low self-esteem will do anything to avoid being on their own. They will make sure family and friends always surround them. They continually use other people to validate their feelings. The bottom line is, they don't like who they are. To spend time on their own should be viewed as a 'treat' as having particular 'me time.'

A person who talks negatively and never says anything good about people is someone who may be suffering from low self-esteem. They can also struggle with unclear boundaries, as they tend towards not being able to say 'No' to people. They only feel validation when they get the approval of others.

LOSS OF-IDENTITY

When we look back at our lives, we can see how the train analogy (Introduction/conclusion) reflects the different stations/stages we pass through in life. Different roles come and go during this journey – i.e. daughter, sister, employee, or carer, etc. Some hopefully stay with us to the end. When circumstances change in our lives, such as when a mother who has devoted all her life to bringing up her children, suddenly finds herself lonely and redundant, as both her teenage sons have left home to attend university, it can be devastating for a woman whose main goal in life was to see to the needs of her kids. The mother will feel she has lost her identity and doesn't know who she is. This empty nest syndrome is prevalent for women when they reach their 40's and 50's.

Although it will be hard at the beginning, instead of concentrating on the loss of being a full-time mother, one should look at this stage of life as an opportunity to do more things as a wife. Maybe it would be a chance to take that long-awaited luxury cruise with her husband.

Loss of identity can hit us also, in other ways too.

In 2004, I was working as a practice manager in a busy doctor's surgery. I loved my job; it was demanding and time-consuming. A day never went past without some different challenge. It could be all the computers had crashed in the building to an unhappy patient who wanted to make a complaint about the shortage of available appointments. I worked long hours, but I loved the role.

However, after 16 years of never taking sick leave, I had to book a day off to go into hospital for elective ENT surgery. The name of the procedure was FESS. Functional Endoscopic Sinus Surgery. I had the surgery booked for Thursday 24th May 2004.

I planned to be back at work the following Monday as I had a packed diary.

I knew I had to take this opportunity to have the sinus surgery as I had been having sinus problems for a long time.

Unfortunately, things did not go to plan. The surgery didn't fix my problem; in fact, it made my sinuses worse. I was re-admitted and had to go through a revision procedure to rectify the problem. When I was coming out of the anaesthetic, I knew instantly that something significant was wrong. The back of my head, neck, and back was in a considerable spasm. In fact, for the next two years, I lived with this level of acute pain daily. I couldn't walk, sit, or move; the pain was excruciating. I was on morphine and tramadol, but nothing took the pain away. My world felt upside down. Instead of being a functional human being with a good career, I was now an invalid who couldn't do anything for myself. I relied on my family to do everything for me.

As the months went on, I became more depressed; I didn't know who I was. I felt useless. I had lost my identity. I didn't know who I was supposed to be. I eventually had to apply for early retirement as my consultant couldn't say how long the pains in my neck and back would last. An MRI had shown up an underlying condition called cervical spondylosis. Although I didn't know I had this condition, however, the twisting of my neck during the second surgery had triggered it to become active.

I'm telling you this story as it's another example of 'loss of identity'. Now that I was no longer a practice manager, I kept asking myself the question, "Who am I now? Who have I become?"

To heal from this situation, I first had to understand who I was outside this status. For instance, I had to accept I was no longer a manager, but I was, more importantly, a mum, wife, and sister, etc. I had to dig deep into my heart to find myself again and realign with what was important. It was a depressively low time for myself, but thankfully, this was a time when my relationship with God began to grow.

Although I couldn't understand it at the time, God had started to work the Pruning Principle in my life. He began to cut out what wasn't useful. According to Vicki Norris, this kind of trimming is helpful as it cuts out what isn't helpful in our life.

The Bible applies the metaphor of pruning to our spiritual life:
'Jesus explains I am the true Vine, and my father is the gardener. He Cuts of every branch that bears no fruit, while every branch that does Bear fruit he prunes so that it will be even more fruitful.'
John 15 1-2

There is no doubt, this period of my life was painful, but somehow I took comfort in God that he had other plans for me.

CHAPTER 2

- THE WEIGHTY EFFECT OF CARRYING GUILT, SHAME, AND REGRET ON YOUR LIFE

A common source of emotional clutter is guilt and shame. These emotions are powerful and usually go hand in hand. However, when we examine them, they are different.

First of all, GUILT – is more about how we feel about ourselves. It's feeling responsible that we may have hurt someone. It doesn't matter if it was real or an imagined action. Guilt also reflects on how we think about ourselves and usually arises as a feeling we may have hurt someone. Guilt is the voice telling us we have done wrong, or we are about to do it.

Guilt is not just about what other people think; it's the condemnation we take on ourselves. It's a heavy burden to carry and only survives in places where you care. That's why guilt is a common emotion when it's tied up with our family and friends. The following story of Mary and her elderly mother is an example of how guilt can affect mental health.

Mary was a 46-year-old married lady. She lived with her husband and elderly mother. They had one daughter, who emigrated to Australia a few years earlier.
Mary's daughter was having her first child and wanted her mother and father to come out to Australia. Mary was reluctant to visit, as she knew her mother wasn't
in good health. However, Mary and her husband made arrangements for her mother to go into respite care while they were away. They thought she would be okay until they came back. Unfortunately, while Mary and her husband were away, Mary's mother took a heart attack and passed away.

Mary came to see me for counselling as she was grief-stricken over the death of her mother. Mary felt so guilty that she had left her mother. She kept beating herself and kept saying to herself, if only she hadn't gone to Australia, her mum would be still alive today.

Mary's feeling of guilt toward's her mother's death is a normal response. She was now living with the perception that she failed her mother as she was now struggling with intense feelings of guilt. She kept saying, 'If only I hadn't gone to Australia, mum would be still alive.'

Mary's feelings of guilt are part of the grieving process. Her conscious was telling her she had been a good daughter to her mother. However, she couldn't move past the obstacle that she wasn't there when she needed her. Mary was disappointed with herself, but she knew herself, no-one could have predicted her mother's death. Even her mother's GP was surprised by her passing. Mary hadn't a crystal ball; she couldn't tell the future. She made the best decision with the information she had at the time. Mary's mother even encouraged her to go to Australia for the birth of her grandchild. Understanding this regret is a good starting point. In this case, it was the fact of not being there at the end when her mother died. Accepting this and understanding this feeling of regret is the beginning of the healing process.

The truth is, Mary knows her mother wouldn't have wanted her to miss out on the birth of her first grandchild.

SO WHAT IS SHAME?

Shame is probably one of the most substantial emotional burdens a person could carry. Unfortunately, people can live their whole life carrying this cumbersome burden around. The person isn't even aware that they are carrying this baggage. Hanging on to worthless emotions is a waste of time as well as energy.

Sadly, when a person suffers from shame and guilt, they are

vulnerable to adopting unhealthy addictions, such as alcohol and drugs, etc. 'Shame' is slightly different from 'Guilt.' When you experience guilt, it's usually about something disapproving you have done. However, when you feel shame, it's triggered by a thought that is telling you that you are an awful person. Together, these emotions are a deadly alliance in the fight against depression.

Again, we come back to the effect of what carrying emotional baggage has on our lives. Shame is up there as one of the biggest loads we carry. A predator of sexual abuse will never own the shame themselves. Unfortunately, it's usually the victim that ends up shouldering the burden.

The abuse of anyone is never fair. There is always an unfair advantage with the abuser because of the power he/she holds over the victim. It could be a parent, step-parent, a cleric, an older relative, even a neighbour. Anyone who holds the power ace in a relationship has an unfair advantage over the victim. The sad truth is that the predator projects blame and shame on to the victim, and then the victim accepts the projection as the truth. Unfortunately, the victim is made to think they brought the shame on themselves. Nothing could be further from the truth as with most of these cases, the balance of power is always with the predator.

CHAPTER 3

- ARE YOU HOLDING A GRUDGE AND CAN'T LET GO THE ANGER?

Actively holding on to a grudge can be physically exhausting. Try looking at the grudge as a big black bag of old rubbish that has been part of your life for years. It's a useless bag; it serves no purpose except it represents a load of old memories that have brought you a lot of pain in the past. You hold tight to this bag; you take it everywhere you go. It's always a reminder for you not to forget these memories and the past hurts that someone did to you.

Even when life goes well, and you feel you have moved on, this black bag that you are holding on to will feel like a lead weight around your neck.

As time goes on, the grudge gets heavier to carry. It makes us feel bitter, angry, jealous, and dissatisfied with life. Even when someone is helpful and kind, we can't enjoy and take pleasure from it, as we cannot forget the old memory. Unfortunately, holding on to the grudge has far-reaching consequences.

ANGER

When a person gets angry, it triggers their fight or flight response. The hormones adrenalin and cortisol are released into the body. Fear, anxiety, and excitement are the primary emotions that trigger the fight or flight response. The effect of these hormones in your body is beneficial, especially if you are about to get mugged as you acquire a surge of energy that helps you to get out of the impending danger.
The previous paragraph explains how anger, when used appropriately, can get you out of a dangerous situation.

However, problems occur when the fight or flight response is triggered not by real physical danger but merely by thought.

When unmanaged anger takes a grip on a person's life, it can also affect their short and long term health. Headaches such as migraines, stomach ulcers, and sleep disorders can occur.

Unhealthy ways to manage anger can reinforce the impact of how it affects the body. Strokes and heart attacks can be the ultimate threat.

Unhealthy ways to deal with anger:
- is to repress the anger/passive aggression

By doing this, you bottle up the anger; you won't talk about it to anyone. Unfortunately, the long-term effect can lead to anxiety and depression.

Passive-aggressive people find it hard to say what they want or mean. If you listen to the words they are saying, they don't mean what they are feeling.

There are two types of passive aggression;
The first is the obvious one (overt). This is where passive-aggression is apparent, i.e., silent treatment ignores and continually gives the cold shoulder.
The other type is (covert); this is when passive aggression is done secretively and not in the open.

The following is an example of covert passive aggression.

Carol worked as an assistant manager for a large retail firm. The company employed her for ten years. For the past five years, she worked alongside the manager in her department. They had a good working relationship until the manager took early retirement due to ill health. Unfortunately, Carol thought she would automatically get promoted. However, the firm had other ideas and decided to advertise the position in the local newspaper. Unfortunately, Carol wasn't successful, and a

23-year-old graduate filled the post. Carol was upset, as she felt the job should have been hers.

Carol found it hard to speak to the new manager, never mind show her the ropes. However, she passed herself as she knew if she obstructed the new manager's induction, she would be in trouble with management. Carol adopted a covert passive aggression behaviour.

Routine Tasks that generally would take Carol an hour to do would now be spread out over days. Carol's work became sloppy. However, it wasn't bad enough to be disciplined. However, it did affect the overall sales figures for the department.
Covert and overt passive aggression is very subtle. It's sometimes quite hard to prove; however, it can turn out to be more of a problem than someone who shows their anger outwardly.

What we must remember is that adopting a passive-aggressive behaviour can be just as damaging to ourselves as to other people. The word passive in this context means to pass over. A person who acts passively is when they allow their needs to be passed over.

The person will feel unable to express their anger, and sometimes they will adopt sarcasm and humour to mask their true feelings.

Anger Rage
The flip side of passive aggression is raging anger, which leads to physical and emotional abuse. Not only do you risk getting into trouble with the law, but it can also affect the relationships you have in your life. If a person doesn't control their anger, they will ultimately drive people away and end up living a lonely life.

As a counsellor, I find the human mind fascinating. I'm not just talking about in the Therapy room, but also when I am out and about.

Sometimes, during my working day, I will take a walk into the nearest shopping mall and call into Starbucks for a latte. I enjoy the relaxation of chilling out after a busy morning. Thankfully, most people around me sit and have an enjoyable catchup conversation with their friends. However, sometimes it's unavoidable to eavesdrop when someone starts talking in a louder than usual voice of how dissatisfying life is. I remember, on one particular occasion, a lady was speaking about her adult children; she kept repeating how horrible one of her daughters-in-law's was. Every time her friend asked her about her grandchildren, the lady would skip over it and start ridiculing her daughter-in-law again. She had never forgiven her for an incident that happened many years previous.

I thought to myself this is typical of so many people's lives. They hold on to so much anger and unforgiveness that it's like cancer growing inside them. The anger is so intense that it overwhelms any good stuff that the person may experience. I'm sure this lady in the coffee shop had beautiful little grandchildren that she didn't appreciate. The grudge she was holding on to took precedence over everything else.

Of course, I'm not dismissive that this lady hadn't cause to be offended. Her hurt may be justified. However, it's what she does with the offence that counts. If we like her hold on to it, moan and talk about it to everyone else but never sit down with the person concerned and explain how the hurt had affected them. The chances are the daughter-in-law may not even be aware of the impact of her actions.

The sad conclusion of this story is the lady in question who has estranged herself from her family may be waiting for an apology that will never come.

The lady in the above example is not alone, so many people who hold grudges, end up living isolated lives. People mistakenly believe that by holding out and not speaking to someone means they are the strong person and the other is the weak one. It couldn't be further from the truth. Keeping a tight hold of that black bag of grudges and unforgiveness brings nothing but grief and loneliness. It can also be a trigger for future mental health and physical issues.

CHAPTER 4

- ARE YOU CLENCHING ON TO UNFORGIVENESS? – HOW IT AFFECTS YOUR SELF-WORTH AND SELF-ESTEEM.

Unforgiveness is a heavy burden to carry. It can affect all areas of one's life. Sometimes, the one relationship that is overlooked is the relationship the person has with himself. If he/she is not happy with who they are, they can suffer low self-esteem issues. It can then sometimes bring neediness and doubt into a new relationship.

In contrast, when two well-balanced people meet, they have a better chance of forming a robust, healthy relationship as they will complement each other.

So many people come to counselling for advice on how they should cope regarding a specific relationship. I.e., an overbearing husband, who continually judges them: a friend who has let them down; a mother who always prefers their sibling instead of them. The list is endless.

Of course, all these relationship issues are essential, but the one that is most significant to me as a counsellor is the one they have with themselves.

I'm intrigued at the responses I get when I start to ask penetrating questions.

Do you like yourself?
Do you feel important?
Do you feel valuable?

Usually, the client looks stunned, as if to say, why are you asking this about me? Do you not realise that I'm not the problem, it's so and so, if it weren't for them, I wouldn't have all this anxiety.

After a period of trying to dodge my questions and talk about everything else under the sun, they do eventually answer. However, it never ceases to amaze me how low an opinion they have of themselves. It's probably the first time they have admitted to themselves that they don't like the person they have become.

However, this is a great starting point for me as a counsellor, as it's the first step towards the client's recovery.

UNFORGIVENESS

I have found that many people would do anything rather than admit they have unforgiveness in their hearts.

The following is the story of Marie, who came to counselling five years after the breakup of her 23-year marriage. Marie was 47 years old. She and her husband were the parents of three teenage girls. Marie's marriage broke up because of infidelity; she discovered her husband was having an affair with his secretary, who was 15 years younger than Marie.

Although many years had passed since the divorce, Marie was still carrying a lot of unforgiveness. When she spoke about her husband, her voice would go into a high pitch rant. Marie was angrier now about her husband's betrayal than she was at the time.

Mary couldn't understand why she was still feeling so low, after so many years. What Marie didn't realise was, she could never be free of bitterness as long as she continued to think unforgiving thoughts. Holding on to the past, no matter how justified she was, was making her ill with resentment.

Marie felt a prisoner to her past. She thought she was giving in and being weak if she started to soften her attitude towards her ex-husband. As the counselling therapy progressed, Marie began to realise that the act of forgiveness takes place in her mind.

It has nothing to do with her ex-husband. Just because Marie would decide to forgive her husband, it doesn't mean that she condoned his behaviour. Quite the contrary, by letting go of the past, she could now start to live in the present.

Marie started to find that by stopping to blame her ex, she began to reclaim her power back in life. In other words, Marie began to choose rather than react continuously.

Marie also found that by starting to think more positively of herself, her self-esteem and self-confidence began to grow. It wasn't long before Marie did more things with her girls. They all began to forge a happier relationship with each other. In conclusion, because Marie became more loving, she became more lovable. Letting go of the burden of unforgiveness has had a massive impact on her life.

CHAPTER 5

- GRIPPED BY FEAR – HOW IT AFFECTS YOUR LIFE?

Fear is, 'An unpleasant emotion or thought that you have when you are frightened or worried by something dangerous, painful, or bad that is happening or might happen.' *https://dictionary. cambridge.org/dictionary/english/fear*

Like all other negative emotions, holding on to fear can have an adverse outcome for your mental health. Fear and anxiety affect different areas of your life; it starts to control what you do and what you don't do.

The fight or flight response is triggered when perceived danger happens. Floods of adrenaline and cortisol get released into the body. Fortunately, when this happens, it can help a person escape an oncoming threat. However, if the danger is not real, and only in mind, it can be the stimulus for anxiety and depression. Regrettably, by listening to this fear-based voice in your head, it will stop you from succeeding and achieving new goals.

By letting go of fears, a person will start to do new things. They will become more excited and passionate about their life. If a person moves out of their comfort zone, they will begin to grow and flourish as a person. They will not fear failure.

Other fears are the fear of losing control, the fear of getting hurt, or even the fear of change. When fear grips a person, they don't function properly. They find rational thinking hard. The mind is like a survival mechanism, which has a goal of keeping you alive. Its primary job is protection. Unfortunately, because it's so diligent, the mind thinks that the only way to protect you is to control everything in your life. The downside of this is that it can be restricting and limiting, as fear keeps you from growth and expansion.

Fear also affects relationships, whether it be your partner or a work colleague. Most people who live a fear-based life are not aware they are acting up. However, the fear of failure tends to operate in the unconscious mind. You are not aware of how it holds you back from having a successful life. It isn't so much the fear of failure that does the damage but the fear of being shamed.

Children are brought up and being taught that getting it right the first time is what success is all about. It's always the first person to get the question correct in the classroom that receives the praise and the prize. Unfortunately, coming second or third is not usually remembered. It has to be the first.

Success based on this premise is quite sad; after all, how many entrepreneurs fail at business three or four times before they get the breakthrough they need. Coming back after a fall is what it's all about. A successful person is one who can spring back into the game after he/she has fallen. The more flexible a person is, the more comfortable they will be able to jump back into the arena. The most triumphant business people in the world are the ones who wouldn't take no for an answer. They keep trying until they succeed.

PART 2

THE NEGATIVE HABITS AND BEHAVIOURS THAT MENTAL BAGGAGE CAUSE

Get to know the types of addictive behaviour
that are less well known

CHAPTER 6.0

– ADDICTIONS ARE NOT JUST SUBSTANCE ABUSE;

OBSESSIVE CONTROL ISSUES;

When the topic of addictions comes up, we automatically assume it concerns substance abuse. The main ones are alcohol and drugs.

As discussed in Part 1, all these addictive and harmful behaviours are in response to the amount of emotional and mental clutter we carry about in our head, namely anger, guilt, unforgiveness, and fear.

However, negative habits and addictions come in many disguises.

Part 2 of this book discusses the addictive habits that are less known. It can be anything from excessive control issues, people-pleasing, and the repeated attraction to toxic people.

Our need to control things that we have no control over leaves us always feeling a failure. There is no way we can control other people's behaviour. No matter how hard we try, it will always end up making us feel anxious and useless.

On the other hand, if we end up in a relationship, and we feel our partner has control issues, how do we recognise it? What are the warning signs?

Take, for instance, Andrea, who was a 25-year-old nurse. She met Alec, who was a 28-year-old freelance photographer on an online dating app. Andrea couldn't believe how fortunate she was as Alec seemed to have all the qualities she ever had wanted in a man. Although she was only dating him a short time, she felt she had known him forever.

At first, Andrea, was quite flattered by Alec's attention. When she was out having lunch with friends, Alec would facetime her and ask what friends were in her company. Of course, Andrea and her girlfriends would have a giggle about this and saw no harm in it. They would tell Andrea, 'He is so into you, this looks the real thing.' Andrea was flattered with all this attention. Alec was the first boyfriend that had shown so much interest in her.

As the months progressed, Andrea started to see less and less of her friends as Alec seemed to dominate any free time she had. He would regularly buy presents and new clothes for Andrea. Initially, this was a dream come true, as Andrea was never spoiled by a boyfriend like this before. However, there was a downside; Alec would quickly go into a rage if Andrea didn't wear what he had bought her. Andrea would find herself wearing what he chose all the time, to keep him in a sweet mood.

As time went on, Andrea found herself walking on eggshells not to upset Alec. Initially, Andrea would make excuses for him as she knew he didn't have a good childhood. Alec's mother walked out on him when he was six years of age. Therefore, Alec's father was left to bring him up on his own. When Alec spoke about his mother, he would always get angry. The more Andrea got to know Alec, the more she realised how needy he was as a person. It got to a stage that Andrea started to catch him snooping on her phone while she was out of the room.

Andre, soon realised she couldn't take any more of this obsessive behaviour. She advised Alec that he should attend personal therapy as he wasn't rational most of the time. Alec, however, was in denial that anything was wrong with him. He denied that his mother leaving him as a child had impacted him. He accepted no ownership of his behaviour and didn't think he needed help.

Although Andrea cared deeply for Alex, she felt she had no option to move on from this relationship.

In the above example, Andrea got out of a controlling relationship before it went any further.

So what other signs are there to look out for if you suspect your partner has control issues:

1. Your partner doesn't ask for your opinion as he prefers his way.

2. He will never accept that he's in the wrong. You find that you are the one always having to apologise even though you know it was his fault.

3. Ungrounded jealousy, you have to report into him regularly; if you don't, he will fly into a rage when he sees you.

4. Wants you to ask for his approval before you decide to do anything. Dictates what you should wear and not wear.

5. He infringes on your freedom; he doesn't respect your boundaries.

6. Talks down to you in front of others.

7. Will turn up unannounced at events, hoping to catch you out on something.

8. Will Isolate you from family and friends. Thinks everyone is trying to come between the two of you.

9. He will get angry and jealous of your past relationships. Finds it difficult to accept that you had a life before him.

10. When you do visit family and friends, you are bombarded with texts and calls from him until you return.

Fortunately for Andrea, she got out of a dysfunctional relationship before it went any further.

This second scenario outlines the story of Adam. Unfortunately, because of Adam's past, he was the one who suffered chronic control issues.

Adam grew up in a middle-class home. He lived with his mother and father and younger sister. At 18 years of age, Adam went to university in London. After university, Adam decided to stay on in London and got a job with a large daily newspaper. Unfortunately, Adam rarely went home as he never really got on with his father. He felt that his father was a bully, who ruled the home with strict authority.

It got to the stage that Adam couldn't wait till he was old enough to fly the nest for good.

Adam made a promise to himself, saying, "No one is going to tell me what to do again." This need for dominance, unfortunately, had a significant influence on how he lived his life. It made Adam feel he had to control everything; if he didn't, it would mean he couldn't be happy. It wasn't long before Adam experienced a pattern of broken relationships leading to anxiety and panic attacks.

Thankfully, through some good advice from friends, Adam started to see a counsellor who helped him deal with this unattainable need for control. By doing this, it allowed him to let go of a lot of the issues he was holding regarding his father.

As you see, if either partner experiences any of these control issues, it ultimately harms the relationship.

I'M A SHOPAHOLIC AND I'M IN DEBT.

Jennifer, a 31-year-old graphic designer, worked and lived in Liverpool. She was originally from Ireland but went to university in Liverpool. After Jennifer graduated, she stayed on in Liverpool and made it her home. Jennifer met David, her boyfriend when she was in the first year of college. The two of them lived together for ten years. However, David came in one day and said he wanted to end their relationship. Jennifer knew the relationship had problems but always thought it would work out somehow. Jennifer was devastated. She was deeply hurt, especially when two weeks after the break-up she saw photographs of David along with a new girlfriend on Facebook. He swore to her there was no one else when he left, now even that seemed doubtful. Also, even if that was true, she still felt betrayed as he was able to move on so fast. Within the year, David then went on to marry his new girlfriend. Jennifer continued with her life as best she could; however, she couldn't stop being angry and bitter at the way things happened.

As the years progressed, Jennifer started to depend on shopping trips to lift her mood. Every time she was emotionally down, she would go shopping to cheer herself up. This pattern became a coping mechanism to escape how she was feeling. If anyone ever asked her how she was doing, Jennifer would say she was doing good. Jennifer lived alone with her cat, Paddy. Paddy and retail shopping were the only things that brought joy to Jennifer's life. There wasn't a day passed that Jennifer wouldn't come home to unpaid bills lying on the hall mat. Somehow, the more Jennifer worried about her financial status, the more she shopped.

Jennifer was still in denial of her shopping addiction until she came home one day, and her beloved cat Paddy was on the floor dying. Instantly, Jennifer scooped her little cat up in her arms and took him to their local vet. The vet discovered that Paddy had a bowel obstruction and needed surgery immediately. Unfortunately, because Jennifer's payments to Pet Insurance had lapsed, the certificate for Paddy's insurance was void. Regrettably, this was a wake-up call for Jennifer as she had to find £1,100 for the surgery herself.

For the first time, she admitted to herself she had an addiction to shopping, and it had to stop. Now that she was no longer in denial of the behaviour, she could, at last, do something about it. As you can't change anything, you deny.

With the help of good friends and support of her Church, Jennifer was introduced to CAP, (Christian against poverty). CAP is a not for profit organisation. They worked alongside Jennifer to help her take control of her finances and got her life back on track.

Jennifer also started counselling sessions. The therapy helped Jennifer let go of the anger and unforgiveness she was holding. She didn't realise how much the baggage she was carrying from her past relationship had impacted her life. In conclusion, Jennifer is now living within her budget and is bit by bit getting her debt paid off. However, the good news is that Paddy the cat is now back living at home with Jennifer fully recovered and healthy.

WARNING SIGNS

So what are the warning signs of a shopping addiction?

1. Have your bags of shopping lying in corners about the house. You haven't even unpacked the stuff up, never mind wearing them.

2. Receive a mood lift when shopping.

3. Lose interest in the items, after you purchase them.

4. You spend your entire paycheque even if you know you can't afford it.

5. You start trying to hide your purchases from your family.

6. You make up lies when challenged about the cost of the item.

7. Your closet is full of clothes that still have labels attached.

8. You stop opening the mail, stack it away, so it's unseen.

9. Stop answering unknown phone calls, in case it's a credit card, or banks, etc., looking for payment.

10. You are secretive about your finances in case you feel judged.

11. Continually spends despite promises to stop.

12. Experiencing relationship problems due to overspending.

13. Go on shopping trips to manage feelings of anger, boredom, and frustration.

14. Accumulating excessive stuff and running out of storage room.

15. A decline in financial security and financial hardship.

16. Experience feelings of guilt and shame.

Jennifer's story outlines the consequences of what can happen when a person ignores red flags. The earlier you identify a problem, the easier it will be resolved.

MY MOTHER IS A HOARDER

Alison, a 28-year-old mother of two, rang one day to ask about counselling therapy for her mother. After the usual introductions, I asked Alison, 'Is your mother ready to get help at this time?' I ask this question because so many friends and family see long before their family member that professional support is required. However, Alison assured me her mother had reached rock bottom and was keen for help. With that said, Alison explained that her mother lived alone as her father had died when she was 13 years of age. Since then, her mother had never been right. Alison went on to say her most significant concern for her mother was that over the years, her mother had become a hoarder. It had got so bad now that she feared for her mother's health and safety. Alison proceeded to say that she took her mother to her GP six months ago, and he prescribed antidepressants, but it hadn't helped. Alison also had made different attempts to clear out her mother's house, even though her mother met it with resistance. It did get sorted temporarily. However, it only lasted for a few weeks.

Once we agreed on an appointment. Alison then asked if it was okay to sit in with her mother for the first session. I said that wouldn't be a problem as long as her mum gave permission. She said that would be okay as her mother knew she would be a bit nervous for the first session.

As promised, Alison arrived with her mother for the first appointment. Alison introduced her mother as Maggie. She was 58 years of age, a widow as her husband passed away 15 years earlier. She went on to say she was left to bring up Alison on her own. However, Alison left their home eight years ago to get married and now has two children aged five and four years.

Maggie's eyes started to fill up when she spoke about her husband's death. She said, 'He took a heart attack and died; it was all so sudden.' Maggie admitted things had never been the same since.

Maggie proceeded to talk about Alison and how bossy she had become. Alison sat on the other chair but did not comment. I asked Maggie, 'Why do you think Alison is bossy?' Maggie replied, 'She keeps trying to get rid of my stuff and says my house is unfit to live in.' I asked Maggie, 'What do you think ... is it unsafe to live in?' Maggie did admit the house was full of stuff, but it was full of things she needed.

Maggie then went on to say how frightened she was of Alison coming into her home again and dumping possessions without her permission. I assured Maggie that nothing would be happening against her will.

Maggie went on to say that she knew things had to change. She knew her home was not the way it should be, but unfortunately, she didn't know where to start.

I asked Maggie, 'What would encourage you to get your house in order?'

Maggie looked at me and then to Alison, 'I would love my grandchildren to be allowed back to visit me.'

Alison interrupted at this time and said, 'Yes, I have stopped the kids coming to see Mum, only because I am afraid her house is a fire hazard. If Mum is willing to try and give therapy a go, I can certainly let the kids back into her home.'

At this stage, Maggie burst into tears. 'Yes, I want to give it a go. I want to see my grandchildren again.

With that said, my work with Maggie involved getting her to talk about her concerns. It also was to help her open up about her late husband. For years Maggie has been stuck in the grief cycle. She never really let go of any of her late husband's possessions. She never wanted to let go of anything. It soon transpired that Maggie's hoarding was a symptom of something bigger. She never really dealt with the grief of losing her husband. That's why it was so important to start the therapy as soon as possible. Included in the treatment, Maggie agreed to do a practical task each week in her home; it could be something simple like clearing out a drawer or emptying a box.

Because family plays a massive role in the recovery of a hoarder, we agreed that Alison should sit in on Maggie's counselling session, every fourth week. By doing this, we could address any concerns that Maggie was experiencing as well as monitoring any progress.

It wasn't long before Maggie started to show signs of improvement. She began to understand herself better; she was able to process her thoughts in a better way. Maggie also learned nothing would take away the happy memories she had *with her husband. By doing this, it wasn't long before she began to let go of stuff that was taking up space in her home.*

Six months after therapy had started, Maggie was a different woman. The home decluttered, her grandchildren and her daughter regularly visited. Even old friends who Maggie hadn't seen for years started to drop by.

Physical baggage, along with emotional baggage, can be so damaging to our well-being. Learning to let go of stuff that is of no longer any use can be a liberating experience.

If a family member is a hoarder, plan a strategy. Don't just move in with a truck and haul all the stuff away. It will only hinder your family member. They will feel out of control and distressed at losing their belongings. Just because we see no value or use for an object, it doesn't mean the object is not important. By combining therapy and family support, most people who hoard will slowly recover and have a healthy functional life.

So how can the Bible help us break free from addictive behaviours?

According to Galatians 5:16

"So I say, walk by the Spirit, and you will not gratify the desires of theflesh. For the flesh desires what is contrary to the Spirit, and the Spirit what is contrary to the flesh. They are in conflict with each other so that you are not to do whatever you want. But if you are led by the Spirit, you are not under the law."

If you are struggling with addiction in your life and think you can't control it. Know who you are in Christ. Start agreeing with God.

Remember if the Spirit leads the person, they will not gratify the desires of the flesh. Therefore, addictive behaviours are less likely.

CHAPTER 6.1 'I FEEL BURNT OUT, I CAN'T GO ON.'

The underlying theme of this book is identifying the different types of emotional and mental clutter that clog and overwhelm the mind. The previous chapters outline the main contributors of the clutter, which include carrying the burdens of fear, guilt, shame, anger, and unforgiveness.

- The prolonged effect of carrying this corrosive emotional baggage has a significant impact on a person's mental health.

- If warning signs are ignored, the threat of burnout is imminent:

BURNOUT

The following are warning signs and symptoms relating to a work environment.

- Feeling exhausted all the time.

- Losing the passion for the job, feeling cynical and short-tempered about the organisation.

- Having a sense of dread about going to work each day.

- Sleep pattern changes, insomnia or broken sleep happening regularly.

- The anxiety of work-related issues has started to affect personal relationships.

- Feeling undervalued and not appreciated at work.

- The workload has increased, but resources to carry it out, have decreased.

- Starting to make mistakes and missing deadlines.

- Habitual loss of personal items, i.e., car keys and mobile phones.

- Misplace of work files, that are needed urgently,

- Daily headaches and skeletal pain.

- Workload starting to pile up. The feeling of been overwhelmed.

- Finding it hard to concentrate.

So what is burnout? The best analogy is a super performance racing car, repeatedly going around a track. The warning lights keep flashing, indicating the fuel is getting low. The vehicle continues ignoring the warning lights until, eventually, the car comes to a halt as it has become empty. Burnout in a person is a bit like this; they keep going until they run out of every last bit of energy. The result is they can't physically or mentally go on.

Work burnout can happen to anyone. However, some occupations are more prone to it than others. Namely: social workers, solicitors, teachers, and anyone who works in retail. Call centres are also stressful occupations, especially if it's a complaints department.

When I first started my working life, as a young girl back in the early '70s, the terminology of burnout wasn't known. The term "burnout" was only coined in 1974 by the American psychologist Herbert Freudenberger. He used it to describe the consequences of severe stress and high ideals in "helping" professions.12 Jan 2017.

A lot has changed over the years, particularly in the workplace. In my parents' day, mothers didn't usually go out to work; their job was to stay at home and look after the children. Generally speaking, it was the father's role to go out and earn money to keep the family. Life might not have been that easy, but it wasn't as busy and pressurised as it is today.

What has changed might you ask? Well, for a start, expectations have got a lot higher for most people. Peer pressure encourages children to want only Brand Labels. Technology gadgets and the latest mobile phone are all part of today's wants. For a family who owned a car back in the 1960/70's, it was a luxury, nowadays most young families have two vehicles, which they take as necessary.

Most young couples now have a standard of living that requires the two parents to work. Unfortunately, all of this comes at a price. The pressure and tension forces Mum, and particularly Dad to work long hours to pay for it.

Burnout doesn't appear overnight; it creeps up on you. You are aware that things are not the way they should be. However, you try to keep going.

Bosses have a habit of pushing employees to the limits, that is if you don't actively stop them. Life, unfortunately, becomes a fast conveyer belt that is hard to get off.

Anita was a 49-year-old primary schoolteacher. She worked for the same school for 20 years. Anita came to therapy as she was struggling with work pressures. She felt undervalued and overworked.

When Anita attended her assessment appointment, her presenting symptoms were panic attacks, low mood, and irritability.

Anita explained that since a new principle was employed, there had been drastic changes that had taken place within the school. Unfortunately, these changes negatively impacted Anita's workload.

Anita was getting to the stage that she dreaded going to work.

She knew she wasn't giving her best to her pupils. Anita felt she couldn't go on, and that's why she decided on some professional help.

My work with Anita was helping her to identify what areas of her working day caused her the most stress. The significant stressor for Anita was her inability to say no to other people. The new principle was always asking Antia to take on extra responsibilities. Her colleagues would also come to Anita first if they wanted favour done. In working with Anita, I wanted her to see that she had rights too.

By saying yes to someone else's request, she was facilitating their agenda and forgetting about her own.

Anita learned it was okay to say No. People may not have liked her answer, but they still respected her as a person.

Burnout as a parent
Sadly, not all children can be brought up with their biological parents. So many grandparents have to step into this role because of mental health issues, divorce, or even tragedy

Whatever the family dynamics are, burnout can happen to parents and guardians alike.

Raising a child is a fantastic experience. However, any parent or guardian will tell you that it comes with its fair share of stress.

Sally, a 42-year-old school former retail manager, first came to see me when her baby was 18 months old. She had been married to her husband John for 20 years. In that time, they had tried numerous IVF treatments. Each one didn't work out until the last one. Finally, Sally had the baby she always dreamed of, but it wasn't long before Sally was starting to struggle with motherhood. The baby suffered greatly from colic and was continually unsettled. She went to her general practitioner, and he prescribed an antidepressant for herself and medication to help the baby's colic. However, nothing seemed to lighten the load. Sally felt she was drowning in everyday chores. She couldn't shake off that feeling of not being a good mother and felt ashamed that she was not able to cope. She felt even more guilt, as she didn't have the extra pressure of having to go back to work, as she had given up her career to be a full-time mum.

My work with Sally helped her understand that no matter what your situation is, it's okay to admit you are struggling and need extra support. It's okay not to be perfect. Sally found that after years of dreaming of being a mum and then having that dream come true, it can be a bit disappointing. In Sally's case, because of the lack of sleep and attending the high demands of a colicky baby, she felt burnt out and frazzled. As time went on, Sally learnt that it was no reflection on her as a mother. Fortunately, Sally asked for extra support from her health visitor and family members. Bit by bit, the baby started to improve, and it wasn't long before Sally began to enjoy the experience of being a mum.

CHAPTER 6.2 'I'M CARRYING SHAME THAT'S NOT MINE.'

1. If shame projects on to a victim, he/she will adopt certain practices. The most obvious ones are making the victim feel it must have been their fault. A particular tactic is convincing the victim that if it weren't for them, the abuse wouldn't have taken place in the first place.

2. Self-deprecating behaviour is when a person critically talks about themselves. It can even pass as a humorous joke. It's a form of belittling or undervaluing oneself.

3. People-pleasing behaviour – seeing to everyone's needs except their own. The person continually looks for validation from everyone to feel good about themselves.

4. Always feeling judged – constructive criticism is interpreted as insulting.

The following is an example of how carrying shame can affect a person's life and well-being.

THE SHAME AFTER ABUSE

David, a 43-year-old accountant, came to counselling because he was depressed. Like a lot of men, he didn't find it easy to talk about himself. Married with two children, aged 10 and 12 years, David had a good career; however, he always felt a failure compared with his two brothers. Both David's brothers were all-round high achievers, not just with academic subjects but with athletics as well. David would belittle himself by saying he was the black sheep in the family as everyone else loved watching sport as well as playing it. However, David had no interest in sport at all.

At counselling, David spoke about his low mood; he said he always felt unworthy and not good enough. David said he still felt the odd one out and never had a feeling of belonging.

As the sessions continued, David started to talk about stories of his childhood. One name that kept coming up in the conversation was a person called Uncle Johnny. Uncle Johnny was a brother of his mother. Although he was now dead, he was always a big part of the family. Uncle Johnny had a particular fondness for David. He and David would visit museums as they both enjoyed history.

It was in contrast to the rest of David's family (including his parents) who regularly went to football matches and athletic competitions.

At first, David felt special. However, all that was to change. Although David was only 11 years of age, he began to start to feel uncomfortable when he was alone with his uncle.

David went on to admit that his uncle started to touch him inappropriately. It went on for a few years. David's uncle always convinced him never to divulge their little secret to anyone.

When David was 14 years of age, his uncle took a massive heart attack and died. All the family grieved over his death. Except for David!

As the years went on, David continued to keep the secret to himself. He felt so ashamed of what took place; he felt responsible even for his uncle's untimely death as if he was somehow to blame.

Thankfully through the counselling process, David began to see and understand all that went on when he was a child. Firstly, it wasn't his fault that his uncle touched him inappropriately. The blame fairly and squarely lay with the uncle. The shame that David carried for years was not his, it belonged to his uncle. Okay, his uncle was now dead, but that doesn't excuse the bad behaviour and abuse regarding what he did to David. Gradually David started to believe this. Thankfully, he then started to feel better about himself. He now knows he was carrying a heavy burden of shame that wasn't his to carry.

CHAPTER 6.3 'FEAR IS RUINING MY RELATIONSHIPS.'

Living daily with fear can seriously damage all aspects of your life. One area that can be affected is Relationships. Fear always makes the person feel on edge, and they are rarely able to relax. The fear of rejection is so real and painful that it can have significant implications on the health status of the relationship.

Prolonged fear can also affect the physiology of the person causing panic attacks, migraines, and high blood pressure.

- Fear of failure usually stops a person from trying new things. It holds you back from meeting and interacting with different people. It prevents you from achieving your personal goals and dreams.

- Fear of failure makes you feel that people will forget about you or not respect you. All of this feeds into low self-esteem and makes you feel unimportant.

- You always tell people you are going to fail. You say this because you don't want people to have high expectations of you so that you won't disappoint them.

- You procrastinate jobs that you are supposed to do. You make excuses for not doing it. By stalling the action, you feel you're protecting yourself from feeling a failure.

- Having a Core belief that specifies, 'You have to get it right the first time,' doesn't allow for second or third chances.

- It can hold you back from forming new relationships. It's so easy for a person to stay in their comfort zone and not take the risk of meeting someone new.

Take, for instance, the story of Sharon, who was a 36-year-old solicitor. Sharon was severely hurt by an ex-fiancé when she was in her twenties. Since then, Sharon had avoided men completely. After some persuasion, a friend insisted Sharon should go on a dinner date with a friend she knew. Sharon was not looking forward to the date. Although she had never spoken to this guy, she did, however, know him by sight. Sharon kept saying to her friend, "He's not my type; it will never work." However, Sharon's friend was insistent that Sharon should still go on a date. Sharon agreed. It turned out that Sharon got on great with her date. It turned out to be a fantastic evening.

To sum up Sharon's story, she is now happily married to her new man and is expecting her first baby in a few months.

I am sharing this story as it demonstrates how holding on to fear can have significant implications for your life. It's so sad that such happiness and opportunities could have passed Sharon by if she had continued to stay in her comfort zone. By overcoming this fear, she had chosen the route of opportunity and growth.

By not allowing fear to dominate her life, it will continue to open up new opportunities.

CHAPTER 6.4 'WHY DO I KEEP BEING A PEOPLE PLEASER?'

Anxiety can be brought on by several different reasons. One of the primary reasons is the habit of wanting approval and validation from everyone around us. We all know that this is an impossible task, so when someone does give us a disapproving look, we fall to pieces.

If we spend most of our days trying to please people, we usually end up exhausted and frustrated.

People-pleasing comes from the fear of rejection and the fear of failure. We feel if we don't agree or say yes, they won't want to be with us, or worse still, they might leave, and we will never see them again. Sounds dramatic; however, it's a genuine fear for many, primarily if stemmed from a relationship where the love shown was conditional.

Children brought up with critical parents tend to suffer anxiety, as they are shown love on the condition that they meet their parents' standards. If, for example, a child did not achieve a particular mark in an exam, the parent could withdraw emotional and nurturing support. Unfortunately, a core belief would be formed, implying you are only loved as long as you make people happy. This false belief would also extend to adulthood and contribute to years of anxiety in trying to accommodate other people's approval. This lack of self-worth becomes an integral part of their personality.

SELF-ACCEPTANCE

Acceptance is a primary goal for most people; unfortunately, when this doesn't happen naturally, the person will attempt to get their validation through people-pleasing behaviour. Learning to be accepting of yourself, is a critical component of being at peace with yourself. There may be areas of yourself that you don't like; however, that's okay.

God accepts us unconditionally; he is non-judgemental and

loves us regardless of our mistakes and flaws. That is why we should be more accepting of ourselves if God can love and accept us as we are; there is no reason why we can't allow ourselves too.

If we continually feel the need to say yes to people, when we mean no, it will be only a matter of time before we become disillusioned and disappointed with them. Usually, because the kindness we show is un-precipitated, it can, in turn, make us feel unfulfilled and miserable.

When a relationship starts to be demanding and intrusive, it's a good time to ask:
"Is this relationship worth my time and effort?"

It may also be an excellent time to reflect and ask, "What is it about me that everyone wants to mistreat me?"

The following are signs to watch out for as it could indicate that you may be a people-pleaser.

1. You hate conflict. When someone asks something you disagree with, you stay silent and don't share what you are honestly thinking. The problem with this is that people will never get to know the true you. You probably won't know who you are either. That is why some people who have high levels of anxiety will openly admit that they don't know who they have become. If someone asks if they are okay, they will not tell the truth as they always want to be liked; they don't want to appear bothersome.

2. A person will never see what they do as good enough. They continually strive for perfection instead of progress. Unfortunately, perfection is hard to achieve; therefore, they will never feel content and happy with themselves.

3. A people-pleaser feels resentment instead of fulfilment when they do a kindness. It will be a sense of duty, rather

than a genuine desire to help.

Eve was a 45-year-old lady who came to see me for counselling; she was feeling anxious and depressed. She had lived with her elderly parents all her life, both her parents had recently passed away, and for the first time in Eve's life, she was on her own. Eve talked about her parents and how she felt guilty that she wasn't even missing them the way she should. It transpired that Eve's mother was a controlling person; nothing Eve ever did was good enough. For years Eve had devoted her life to be the carer of both her parents. Eve would do a lot for her parents as she felt it was her duty, she resented being taken for granted but feared ever displeasing them; it meant so much for them to approve of her.

Eve explained, she was feeling numb, she didn't know who she was! Or even what she wanted. Eve had spent years seeing to the needs of her parents; she had somehow lost who she was.

Thankfully through a serious of continuous counselling sessions, Eve began to realise that her needs were essential, it was okay to start looking after herself, it was okay to do what she wanted. Even though Eve's parents were no longer alive, they still had a significant influence on how she led her life. Therefore, it took a while for Eve to accept that it was okay to look after herself. It wasn't long before she went out and met new people. She started travelling, and for the first time in her life, she was who she wanted to be. Eve was, at last, being her own best friend.

People-pleasing is potentially an unhealthy behaviour pattern, starting to let go of it is not easy. Start first by permitting yourself to be able to say, "No." By doing this, other people will begin to get to know the true you. It will surprise you how much they will be able to relate and connect with you better.

CHAPTER 6.5 'I KEEP SAYING YES WHEN I MEAN NO.'

It's incredible how many people live their lives to suit other people. They are so afraid to speak up and say what they need. They go along with what others want.

Take, for instance, Rebecca, an accountant, who came to counselling when she was 26 years old. Rebecca explained she was engaged to be married. Her fiancé was the son of her parents' best friends. The families were not only friends but were business associates as well. The families always encouraged the relationship and loved the fact that the marriage would unite the families even more.

All sounded great; however, when Rebecca came on her first counselling session, it soon became transparent that not all was as it should be. Rebecca started to talk about her life; she explained how fortunate she was at being brought up in a home that she never wanted for anything. Her parents always got the best for her. She also explained how excited her parents were at the forthcoming marriage. However, Rebecca's face didn't show the same enthusiasm. I asked Rebecca why she had now decided to come to counselling. Rebecca burst into tears and explained she wasn't looking forward to her wedding. She just wanted all the anxiety and tension she was experiencing to go away. Rebecca's parents knew she wasn't feeling great, but they just put it down to pre-wedding nerves. After a few weeks of therapy, Rebecca started to feel more comfortable in the sessions; she began to open up more about her life. She explained her mother was controlling, and she thought she always had to do things to keep her happy. Rebecca also admitted that she hated all the fuss of the wedding, but more importantly, she wasn't too sure if it's what she wanted. Rebecca explained she had left it too late now to do anything about it. She was, however, more afraid to admit to her mother than anyone else that she was having second thoughts. My work with Rebecca was to help her find herself, help her see that her needs were essential, but more importantly, to be able to speak them. Bit by bit, Rebecca started to regain her power; she began to realise that this was her life, and it was up to her to say what she wanted and didn't want. It wasn't long before Rebecca informed me that she had a long chat with her fiancé, and they had both agreed to postpone the wedding. She admitted her parents were not happy. However, they have had to accept it. Rebecca realised that throughout her life, she had a habit of saying "Yes" when she meant "No." She always felt it was her duty to always do the right thing and make others happy.

Rebecca learnt, however, that she had rights too, and she was allowed to say "No" if that's what she wanted. Rebecca is a lot happier; she is still not sure whether in the long term the relationship is right for her. However, the most important thing is that she has given herself time; she has taken control of her life and not allowed herself to be influenced by what others want.

Saying Yes when we mean No, affects us all. Usually, if we say yes, we want to please the other person. Unfortunately, this short term gain turns into long term pain.

Saying yes when we mean no can also affect our occupation. The workplace is another example;

As with many therapists, counselling usually comes as a second career. I was no different as my first career was in management/administration. As I said earlier, for 16 years, I worked as a practice manager in a busy health centre. I loved my job; however, it didn't come without its stresses. Robust protocols and rules are followed for the health centre to function correctly.

The main objective of my working day was to meet the needs of patients. In other words, they were able to have an appointment with their GP at a designated time within a safe and comfortable environment.

For this to happen, keeping an adequate level of staff on duty was imperative, especially during busy holiday periods. It's during these favourite holiday seasons that staff always wanted to be off at the same time. Of course, you couldn't blame them as they all wanted to spend time with family. In most cases, through negotiation, something was always sorted out.

However, there were different times over the years that you could not bend the rules. A certain quota of staff had to be on duty, and that was that. I, as the manager, had to say No to staff requests.

Can you imagine the consequences if every one of your staff came asking for the same holiday, and you agreed, it would be absolute mayhem.

The moral of this story is don't be afraid to say NO. Of course, staff will be annoyed by not getting the holidays they want. However, it's more important to be fair-minded and consistent in your decisions. It will also help to show clear boundaries to everyone in the organisation.

CHAPTER 6.6 'WHY AM I DRAWN TO TOXIC PEOPLE?

A new client had just entered the therapy room. After the usual introductions, she sat down. She was in her thirties, and her name was Martha. She was a pretty lady, dressed very smart. However, she kept looking downwards. When she did raise her face, I could see her eyes were red and swollen as if she was crying.

After the completion of the initial paperwork and assessment, Martha proceeded to talk about the reason why she wanted to come to counselling. There were a few issues. However, the main one was the relationship she had with her partner.
Martha explained that she was with her partner for five years. During that time, her partner had cheated on her three times. Each time Martha forgave him and took him back.

Martha's reason for giving in and taking her partner back was that he would cry and blame everybody except himself. He would also blame Martha for his infidelity; he would say she was cold and unresponsive and that her behaviours drove him to look for comfort in other women.

For a while, Martha took what he was saying seriously. She knew herself she could shut down emotionally at times. She tried to make things better by always being there for him. Martha would choose not to meet friends or family often, as she knew these were the sort of things that her partner didn't like.

However, Martha had just found out her partner was having an affair with a co-worker. This time Martha was devastated. Martha had given everything, but it was still not good enough.

Martha proceeded to say that this wasn't her first time of being hurt in a relationship. She admitted that any serious relationship she ever had, ended up with her being hurt and betrayed.

Martha's story is not uncommon. So many people find themselves in the same situation.

The big question is, why is it that some people keep attracting toxic people? Why does this happen?

There can be a few reasons for this. Firstly, it could be an incident earlier in their life. They could have got hurt or bullied. Unfortunately, If the trauma of the event was not appropriately processed, it could have an impact on the person's self-worth and self-confidence. Or maybe they had a controlling father or mother who wasn't able to connect emotionally with them.

Unfortunately, as the person gets older, there are tendencies to be drawn to relationships that have similar traits.

Without stopping to think of the consequences, they continue to let more toxic people into their life.

CHAPTER 6.7 'WHY DO I INTENTIONALLY WRECK MY LIFE WHEN THINGS ARE GOING GOOD?'

One other behaviour that can also sabotage your life is self-limiting beliefs. If you asked the average person what their self-limiting beliefs are, they would probably look at you with a puzzled face. However, holding on to self-limiting beliefs can have significant implications on a person's life. It's the one thing that can stop them from succeeding and attaining their goals.

- So what is a self-limiting belief? Quite simply, it's a story that we tell ourselves in our head.

- So how can a limiting belief be identified?

- Look at an area of your life that dissatisfies you.
If you don't feel you can do anything to change it, then this may be an example that you are carrying a limiting belief.

- We learn our belief systems when we are little children. As we grow older, we create different experiences to match our beliefs.

My own life is a reminder of this. I was born into an average working-class family. My mum and dad were hardworking; I remember dreaming as a child how lovely it would be to attend a university someday and gain a professional qualification. That was just a daydream of a little child. At the age of 11years, my mum decided not to enter me into the 11+ transfer test to attend the local grammar school. I was disappointed, but she felt it was above my capabilities. Whether it was or not, is another question. However, this became a limiting belief in myself, and it went on to become the bedrock of school life. I never pushed myself too much as I never felt I was academically equipped. Although I was fortunate to have loving and caring parents, I still repeatedly told myself that I wasn't very bright. Thankfully, as I grew into adulthood, I became hardworking and always managed to get well-paid jobs. By doing this, and by challenging the old limiting belief I had of myself, I started to believe that it was possible to aim for higher goals. I took the plunge and enrolled myself at the local university for a Hons business degree. Then, in later life, to facilitate a second career, I completed a Masters In Counselling and Communication. What was I starting to do? I was starting to rewrite my story. I was beginning to believe I had the power to start a new narrative. I could see the old story wasn't right. I could see that by hard work and commitment, I had the power to turn around and change my life.

CHAPTER 6.8 SELF-HARMING – 'WHAT MAKES ME DO IT?'

Whether you self-harm yourself or you have a friend or family member who self-harms, it's a hard concept to understand. Why would anyone consciously hurt or give themselves physical pain?

Our rational mind cannot make sense of it. However, the statistics tell us differently. *According to the 7th edition of the Good Childhood Report, produced by UK charity The Children's Society, it states that 22% of 14 -year-old girls in the United Kingdom self-harm.'*

It also states that there is a strong link between general happiness with life and depression. About 47% of children who reported low happiness in life had depressive symptoms. Girls were generally found to be less happy and have more depressive symptoms than boys. The report used the term "self-harming" to describe a wide range of behaviours, including drug and alcohol abuse, as well as physical self-harming.

One of the main recommendations of the report was to ask children themselves how they feel about their lives, rather than rely on observations and assumptions made by adults. Also, the report suggests we shouldn't just look for mental health issues when identifying children in need of support, but also consider their general happiness.' The Good Childhood Report 2018'.

The evidence confirms that self-harming is a real threat to many young people.

So what purpose does the self-harming serve?
According to John Bowlby's attachment style, a child who develops a poor attachment style may be prone to mental health issues later in life.

A child who doesn't develop a secure attachment will find they are fearful most of the time. They have found out from an early age; if they cry and need attention, no one will come to help. No one will be there to sooth them. Unfortunately, this is why a person could easily fall into the habit of self-harming behaviours. The person would know how to deal with physical pain (i.e., put a plaster on the cut) but not mental pain. By inflicting pain and cutting themselves, they would feel they have taken control of their pain. However, they will only feel satisfied for a short period until the emotional pain reappears.

CHAPTER 6.9 I NEED HELP - I'M IN A CO-DEPENDENT RELATIONSHIP

In order to identify a co-dependent relationship, we first have to know what codependency means:

> Codependency is a behavioural condition in a relationship where one person enables another person's addiction, poor mental health, immaturity, irresponsibility, or under-achievement. Among the core characteristics of co-dependency is an excessive reliance on other people for approval and a sense of identity
> *https://en.m.wikipedia.org/wiki/Codependency*

So how do we know if you are in a co-dependent relationship? Co-dependency issues are not always easy to recognise. A person could be in a relationship for years and think nothing of it. It's their normal, its what they are used too. However, at some stage, the person starts to struggle with how they feel about themselves. They begin to question who they really are. They find they live only to please their partner. They only feel validated when their partner is pleased with them. In fact, the fear of disapproval and rejection from their partner means they can never say no to them. This, unfortunately, has a significant impact on that person's self-esteem and self-worth.

This is why certain people are only drawn to partners who appear to have a lot of drama in their lives. A healthy relationship could be possibly boring for them as they wouldn't feel needed. So the needier a person is, the more attractive they are to someone who is a rescuer or a fixer.

The problem with this is the person who has the co-dependency issues can't get past the fact that they are entitled to have their needs met too as they only feel accomplished and validated when they fix them or sort out their partner's problems. If for some reason, their partner gets stronger and less needy, the co-dependent partner will start to feel redundant and worthless within the relationship.

So how do we know if we are in a co-dependent relationship? The following are indicators of what to look out for:

1. Do you always feel it's your responsibility to make everything right for your partner? Is it your job to solve any problems?

2. Do you keep quiet to avoid arguments? Are you the one who always gives in and forgets about your needs?

3. You only feel of value when you are fixing the person and making things right for them.

4. Do you sacrifice everything to keep the relationship going as you feel unworthy to go it alone?

5. Do you have a hard time trusting yourself?

6. You can't identify who you are; you don't know how you feel at times.

7. Do you only feel important when the other person is in trouble, and they come looking to you for help. This is the only time when you feel validated?

8. Do you think you have no say in your relationship?

9. Do you pretend that the choices your partner has made are also your choices? In fact, in reality, it's nowhere near what you would really want.

10. Do you recognise unhealthy behaviours in your partner but stay with them in spite of this?

11. Do you feel it's always the needs of your partner that have to be met and never yours?

12. Do you find that getting approval from your partner is an

integral part of your self-worth and identity?

13. Do you support your partner at the cost of your own emotional, mental, and physical health

A healthy relationship is when there is a balance of shared power. This gives both parties the opportunity for growth and decision-making.

The following case study is an example of what a co-dependent relationship is:-
Jim, a 49-year-old teacher, came to counselling suffering from a lot of panic attacks. Jim said his anxiety seemed to be getting worse. He knew his work was stressful, but he loved being a teacher.

Jim admitted his marriage was not without its problems. His wife Mary was a good woman, but everything had to be on her terms. He felt it was his duty always to meet her needs. Jim felt his only value in the relationship was to make things right and fix things for his wife to be happy.

Over the years, it was Mary who decided where they should live, where they should go on holiday. She even decided that Jim should be a vegetarian like her. She also chose what hobbies she thought was right for Jim. To keep the peace, Jim went along with everything. He knew if he openly challenged any of her decisions, there would be a full-blown row. Jim realised a long time ago that it didn't pay to have an opinion; therefore, it was easier just to go along with what Mary wanted.

However, Jim was at a stage of his life that he was unhappy with whom he had become. He felt, apart from his work, he had lost his identity.

My work with Jim was to start helping him find himself again. Helping to build his self-esteem and for him to start believing that his needs were essential too. Eventually, Jim did get stronger and started to believe in himself again. He even was able to convince Mary to attend a professional couple counsellor together. Thankfully, the couple counsellor was able to confront the codependency issues within the relationship.

The last time I spoke with Jim, he said he was in a much happier place within his marriage. In fact, he said with pride, "I am no longer a vegetarian."

PART 3

TECHNIQUES AND TOOLS USED TO HELP LET GO OF MENTAL BAGGAGE

- Will challenge everything you thought was true.

CHAPTER 7.0

HOW TO DISCARD/CHALLENGE DISTORTED BELIEFS?

Analyzing our core beliefs is not easy. If we live our lives with distorted core beliefs, it will hold us back from living a fulfilling life. That's why it is so essential to make sure our core beliefs are accurate. It also helps us to know the origin of the core belief.

The following are two examples of how a negative core belief develops. CORE BELIEF 'THE WORLD IS A DANGEROUS PLACE'. - Can have a ripple effect on all areas of our life. Because fear is the driving emotion, we have to challenge this fear and ask how true it is. We also have to ask where it originated. We will look at Anne and how this negative core belief affected her life.

Anne grew up in Northern Ireland in the '70s and '80s. At this time, the troubles were at its worst. Every evening bombs would explode. On many occasions, the blasts would vibrate through their tiny home. Anne and her family rarely left their house as they didn't want to be caught up in a bomb alert. As time moved on in Ireland, things began to change. Instead of the regular sirens of blue lights every night, a form of peace had started to take place. People began to go back to normal living, like a visit to the local cinema or a lovely meal out at a restaurant in the centre of town.

Unfortunately, Anne, like many other people, found it hard at first to change that core belief, which is: The world is a dangerous place'.

In later years, Anne would sometimes find herself going into a panic attack if she heard a flashing blue light siren. Instead of believing the core belief that formed when she was a child 'the world is a dangerous place,' she would, with the help of therapy, start to challenge that belief and would say she was safe to go outside as there was no threat to her. The sound of the blue siren was probably a car accident or someone who needed medical attention on their way to the hospital.

It's so important to live your life by accurate core beliefs. If you don't, you are missing out on new experiences.

Core Belief: I SUFFER FROM DEPRESSION. THEREFORE I AM NOT A TRUE CHRISTIAN. This core belief affects our emotional health as well as our spiritual health. *Alice was 28 years of age when she first came to counselling. She was an only child, a born again believer, and still living with her parents at home. Alice also worked for a large IT organisation and had recently worked hard to achieve a sought after promotion. Alice was also an active member of her church and regularly sang in the Sunday morning choir. Unfortunately, throughout Alice's life, she suffered from bouts of depression and was on antidepressants prescribed by her general practitioner. Sometimes the depression would go away, and life was good. However, she felt it was always just around the corner, waiting for the chance to jump back into her life. On her first appointment with myself, Alice started to disclose how unhappy she was. Not only with the depression, but she felt such a fraudster. I asked, "Why do you feel a fraudster, Alice?"*

Alice looked up at me and burst into tears. She said, "I am ashamed of myself. Here am I supposed to be a Christian. I have given my life over to the Lord, but I feel judged by everyone. I feel everyone is saying, how can she be a Christian when she is so miserable all the time. I am starting to believe I am not a true Christian myself; how can I be when I feel this way?"

Alice was finding it difficult to understand why she was feeling depressed as a Christian. Firstly, we have to realise that although we may have given our life over to the Lord, we are still living in this fallen world. We are still affected by what is around us.

We are all taught by society that if we pursue happiness, we will become happy. However, the Bible doesn't share that assumption.

According to Psalm 1:2,3.

Blessed is the man who does not walk in the counsel of the wicked, or set foot on the path of sinners, or sits in the seat of mockers. 2. But his delight is in the law of the LORD, and on his law, he meditates day and night. 3. He is like a tree planted by streams of water, yielding its fruit in season, whose leaf does not wither, and who prospers in all he does.

Thankfully we know the truth about this world, we know it's groaning, and it will come to an end, even those who love the Lord we will groan inwardly until the Lord comes back and a new world is formed.

In conclusion, when a believer looks around this world and sees the mess it's in, we are quite right in seeing the negativity of it. Sadly this belief is not distorted; it is accurate. However, by choosing the Lord's path, we will maintain a greater and wider hope for the future. The Joy of the Lord will continue to refresh us when we journey along with this broken world.

By learning to relax and just do our best, will have a significant impact on our mental health. No one needs to be a superhero. It might just mean tweaking our work schedule by a few hours each week. However, one thing is sure, don't keep going down a road that is filling you with anger and resentment. Prioritise, look at what's essential to your life and work towards that.

THE LESS YOU OWN THE MORE YOU HAVE

The less you own, the more you have! How can this statement be true? It contradicts everything we know in the 21st Century. We are brought up in today's society brainwashed that the more stuff we own, the more successful and happy we are. Research studies contradict this theory, stating that people who are materialists are more than likely to suffer from low self-esteem and low self-worth than those who are not materialistic. So what is materialism? And what impact does it have on our lives today? Firstly, to identify a materialist person, you will first notice they attach their happiness, self-worth, and success to the things they own or buy. It won't matter if they need or can afford them. What matters is that others will think of them in a certain way if they own it. Sadly this is one of the main reasons why people get into consumer debt because they keep buying more and more stuff. Apart from the dopamine rush at the beginning, the newness of the item. I.e., new car, big house, latest technology gadget, it all quickly wears off. So when is enough, enough? Because the person's identity and happiness are dependent on what they buy, the vicious cycle will continue.

So how can we start changing our attitude towards materialism?

The first step is to start being honest with yourself. As outlined in Part 1 of this book, losing your identity and not knowing who you have become can have a detrimental effect on your mental health. Therefore, start focusing on things that matter, then the things that you need will come anyway. Continue to focus your mind by saying 'I have enough!'

Instead of focusing your happiness on material things, start focusing on the experiences that take place with family and loved ones. Remember how important it was to see your child's first step! Remember the tender moment when your boyfriend first told you he loved you. Remember how proud you were on your daughter's graduation day when she walked up to the podium to accept her hard-earned degree. Money can't buy these sorts of experiences.

Learn to savour the moment, and the memory will be there forever.

HOW TO HELP A HOARDER, DON'T HINDER THEM

I have to admit; I personally am a bit of a minimalist. I try not to hold on to anything that is of no longer any use. I like my home to be clutter-free and organised. In other words, I don't feel the need to fill space with stuff. In saying that, I am not an advocate of having the austere and spartan look either.

So what is hoarding? How do we know if we have a problem? First of all, the person will rarely identify their hoarding as a problem. It's usually a family member who initially highlights it. The level of hoarding can vary from mild to severe.

So how do we go about trying to help a family member who is living in chaos? How can we approach them without them getting defensive and angry? Just like Maggie in chapter 6 Maggie felt violated and disrespected when her daughter Alison attempted to clear out the clutter without permission. This type of approach will alienate the person from her family as well as only being a short term solution to the actual hoarding.

Nonetheless, hoarders can recover if they have the right support system in place.

The following are steps and strategies that will help your family member work towards a permanent recovery from hoarding:

1. The first step is to try and sit down with the family member and discuss the impact their home is having on their life. Try and not judge, but highlight what the person is missing. (It's so crucial at this stage to highlight the motivation for recovery.) Like Maggie's story, she had to do without the visits from her grandchildren. By doing this, it will help the person move away from their usual denial behaviour.

2. Assure your family member that you won't be doing anything without their permission. However, this is an excellent time to ask the family member to start having personal therapy. Encourage them that this will give them a chance to talk to someone objective who won't judge.

3. The therapist will explore the underlying issues related to hoarding, which can range from past trauma, grief, or fear of losing control, etc.

4. The therapist will help the client become more self-aware. She will also help with the decision-making process, which in turn will help the client challenge the distorted views of what to hold on to and what to let go.

5. Along with the client, the support network, i.e., family members, the therapist, or even the social worker, can attend regular meetings to monitor progress.

6. Assign practical tasks for the client every week: e.g., clear out a drawer; nothing too big, everything in little steps.

7. When the client is ready, and trust has started to build up, family members can come and help the client to start the decision making on what to keep and what to let go.

8. The family can organise practical aids for the decluttering. I.e., large bin bags, labels marked: CHARITY SHOP, RUBBISH, TO BE KEPT, or even to hire a skip for the outside.

9. When decluttering, remember to respect the person's decision to keep a specific item. It's good always to coax them to stay realistic on why they want to keep it.

By continuing to keep a healthy dialogue with the family member, it will keep reminding them of all the advantages of living in a home that is safe, clutter-free, and organised.

CHAPTER 7.1 BE THE PERSON YOU WANT TO BE - HOW TO VALIDATE YOURSELF BY SELF APPROVAL

If you have a poor relationship with yourself, the good news is that you don't have to stay that way. It may take a bit of work on yourself, but it will be worth it.

1. Start letting go of Perfection. A perfectionist's life is always living with a sense of disappointment. Sometimes when a person is brought up in a critical household, they tend to believe they have to be perfect to be loved. Everyone knows this is not a perfect world we live in. So nothing you do will be perfect. Letting go of perfection is a healthy decision to make. Reframing your internal dialogue by saying, 'I did the best I could, I am proud of what I achieved,' is far healthier.

2. Avoid comparing yourself with others. It's so easy to fall into the trap that everyone has a better life than yours. Accept that everyone is different. Everyone suffers from some degree of stress. It's just that some have better and healthier coping mechanisms than others.

When a person starts to be less critical of themselves, they will soon begin to reap the benefits of how they view themselves. They will begin to validate themselves. In due course, their self-esteem and self-confidence will increase.

If a person continually lives their life adopting a passive style of communication, there is a good chance they will be storing up trouble for the future mainly because the person will continually sacrifice their own needs for those of others. On the other hand, if a person adopts an aggressive style, they will project themselves as hostile and may even be labelled as a bully.

Either end of this spectrum is unhealthy. Therefore, the object is to aim towards the middle of the spectrum. A person will then communicate in a healthy, assertive manner.

It is vital to always aim towards the centre of the spectrum; this way, you are not too passive and not too aggressive. You will be speaking positively. Being assertive is a skill that needs practice. There will be times you will be better than others; however, you can always learn from your mistakes. The great advantage of using assertive language, you will have a better chance of getting what you want.

By being assertive, you will portray yourself with an air of confidence as you will express yourself without being passive or aggressive.

STEPS TO BECOME MORE ASSERTIVE

The following are essential steps to becoming more assertive:

1. Listen - Listen carefully; don't interrupt the other person. Don't be dismissive of what they say. Try to understand the other person's point of view. You might not agree with what they are saying. However, you still should be respectful of what they are saying.

2. The tone of voice - The tone of voice is fundamental. If you speak in a soft clear voice, the other person will listen to you better as you will not sound hostile. When a person shouts or raises their voice, even if what they are saying is correct, the other person will immediately switch off.

Try to speak in a manner that is simple, direct, and concise. Don't over complicate your answer by going off on a tangent. Keep to the topics discussed. In other words, keep it simple.

3. Try to relax - Even though the topic discussed might be serious, still try to be as calm and relaxed as possible. Take deep breaths and relax; this will also help you to be more confident. Give good eye contact and sit in a relaxed position that you feel comfortable; this will also help the other person to be relaxed as well.

4. Boundaries - All relationships need boundaries. You don't want people to take advantage of your caring nature any more than letting them think you are aggressive and a bit of a bully.

You want people to know the true you. You want them to feel relaxed in your company. However, you want them to respect your rights as a person and not take advantage of you.

Setting boundaries will empower you to know when to say No and also to when to say Yes.

5. Unhealthy Sentence Starter - If you get annoyed with your partner, how many times have you started a sentence with YOU. E.g. –
'You always do that.'
'You never think about me.'
'You are always late.'
'You don't care about me.'
'You always drive too fast.'

I suppose we are all guilty of these sentence starters to some degree. The problem with starting a sentence with 'you' indicates to the other person that you are beginning to judge and accuse them; this will make them feel they have to defend themselves, and they will become defensive. Try and eliminate the 'You' sentence starter as much as possible. For alternatives sentence starters. Begin with I … I feel nervous when you drive fast. I feel sad when you come home late and neglect to ring … I feel angry when you say things like that …

CHAPTER 7.2 FINDING FREEDOM IN NOT BEING A PEOPLE PLEASER

- A person who feels it's their job to keep everyone happy will sooner or later run into problems. The problem with this way of thinking, it's always about everyone else and not about you. You end up putting up with things that may be against your values and integrity. When you put yourself out to please others, you are not the true you. People around you may not ever get to know who the true you is. In other words, you end up misleading them instead of pleasing them.

- A common consequence of a people pleaser is to feel lonely as you are not allowing people to connect to your true self.

- To stop being a people pleaser, we first have to draw a line on how we did things in the past. The following six steps are how to go forward and stop being a people pleaser.

1. Stop letting others make the decision. When a friend asks you out for lunch, you are entitled to suggest a place of your liking too. Start practising by saying:
'How about we try that new restaurant that has opened in the High Street.'

2. You are allowed to have an opinion. If you work in a stuffy office and one colleague decides to keep the windows shut. You can say, I know it's a bit draughty, but if you don't mind, I am going to open the window for half an hour.'

3. Don't forget your needs are essential too. Saying Yes is a habit. Start to practice by saying small No's. Give yourself time by stalling an answer, such as I'll let you know by email at the beginning of next week.'

4. Start being honest with what you really want. If you are in a relationship and you know it's going nowhere, rather than waste any more time, you could say the following,
' Thank you for some lovely memories, but we both know

that it's time for us to go our separate ways.' Although such statements may sound harsh, however in the long term you are doing not only yourself a favour but also the other person too. You are facing up to the reality that if something is not working, there is no point continuing.

Through time the other person will appreciate your honesty. You will also feel better yourself as you are taking charge of your life and not letting it drift.

5. Finally, stop apologising. You are doing nothing wrong. You are starting to stand up for yourself and taking control of your life. Accept that not everyone will like you. Accept you are not going to be all things to all people. Start to speak up; let people know if they have done something to upset you. Find your VOICE, and you will start to find your true self.

CHAPTER 7.3 FINDING CONFIDENCE IN SAYING 'NO THANK YOU.'

- Start giving yourself permission to say No. If a person feels they have the RIGHT to ask something from you, remember, you have the same RIGHT to be able to say 'No, thank you.'

- Keep your explanation brief. Of course, be courteous, but don't go into a lengthy apology on why you are saying No. Remember it's okay to say No.

- Above all, don't feel guilty; remember your needs and values are essential. It's good you respect your values and that you don't compromise on anything that will make you feel bad. Be proud of who you are.

- When you say No to a person, remember it's not you they don't like, it's the request that you turned down that displeases them. They will probably respect you more for your honesty.

- Ask yourself – is this what I want? Instead of rushing in and saying Yes – postpone and say 'I'll get back to you.'

- Stand your ground, saying Yes also says no to something else.

- If you feel that you do want more time to think about it, use: 'I'll ring you next week and let you know.'

CHAPTER 7.4 REACH FOR THE SKY AND MAKE YOUR DREAMS COME TRUE.

Start by getting an understanding of what is making you fearful and what's holding you back. Address the underlying core belief; for instance, the core belief of 'A person needs to get it right the first time.' The following explains the impact of believing a distorted core belief relating to failure and how it affects a person's life. *Living with this core belief can be self-limiting, for example: Carol was a 30-year-old divorced lady. She works in her family's retail business. Unfortunately, Carol and her husband separated a few years after their marriage. She caught her husband having a string of affairs. Carol felt the marriage could not continue, so she filed for divorce. Since then, Carol has lived an isolated life; she rarely ever left her home. Carol felt ashamed that her marriage didn't work out. She felt a failure and an embarrassment to her family. Carol was brought up in a family that divorces didn't happen. Her family were all high achievers, and nothing ever seemed to phase them. Since Carol was a little girl, one of her core beliefs was, 'You have to get it right the first time'. Living by this core belief always meant that Carol had only one shot at getting something right. Therefore, because Carol's marriage failed, it felt her whole life was a failure.*

So when Carol first came to counselling, she presented with low mood, low self-esteem, and a deep-rooted fear that the best of her life was over. She felt she had her chance for happiness, and it hadn't worked out.

My work with Carol started by challenging this distorted core belief that if she didn't get things right the first time she was, in fact, a failure. I began to ask Carol the areas of her life that made her proud. Carol didn't realise until she rhymed them off how many accomplishments she had. For example, she was a great singer; she could play several instruments, she had won some tennis tournaments, never mind being a great help to her parents in running the family business. We talked about the breakdown of her marriage. Instead of feeling a failure, she started to realise that sometimes things don't work out the way we would want, but that's okay. However, instead of giving up, we are to learn from what happened so that we can move on.

Carol agreed that on reflection, she ignored red flags before her wedding day, that all was not right with the relationship. Bit by bit, Carol started to get emotionally stronger, she learnt to address problems, rather than overlook them, especially if it's a new relationship,

Eventually, Carol began to date again. At last, she felt she wasn't a failure. She felt confident about her future as she has learnt a lot about herself.

CHAPTER 7.5 HOW TO RECOVER FROM BURNOUT AND BECOME STRONGER THAN EVER.

PARENTAL BURNOUT

Whether your child is a newborn or a teenager, being a parent doesn't come without its stresses.

- In Sally's situation, the first instance is to get some normality back into her life. It's okay to admit you are not okay. Help is out there, whether it be your GP, health visitor, counsellor, or a family member.

- Identify the triggers, stabilise them first to avoid burnout.

- Start having a new mindset that your needs are essential. If you are suffering sleep deprivation, no wonder you're feeling tired and lethargic Sleep is crucial to a person's well being as it's the one thing that balances a person's mood.

- Ask a family member to babysit for a few hours, even if it's just for you to go shopping or maybe a catchup coffee with an old friend.

- A lot of young mothers feel guilty that they don't want to be with their child 24/7. It's okay to have. "Me time." You must have that protective time set aside for you alone.

- I always refer back to the aeroplane analogy. When an emergency occurs in mid-air, the oxygen masks are released. The onboard instructions for mothers are, to make sure your mask is secure before you see to your child. This simple instruction also relates to everyday life. You cannot help others if you first are not okay. In that way, no matter what role you play, whether it be a mum, daughter, wife, employee, you will be able to give it your best as your basic needs are met.

- Adding new norms and rituals to your daily routine will

ensure this.

- Above all, remember this world is not a perfect place to live in, so you don't have to be perfect; you do your best, that's what's important.

Social Media has proven to be a real source of discontentment. A mum who is already feeling overwhelmed and unsupported with her life feels even more dissatisfied and exhausted when she sees other people's families look picture perfect on social media. Again 'too much' available information can hurt our well-being. Always remember, these happy family photos are only a glimpse of a second, into a person's life. They like you have their share of stresses and problems.

WORK BURNOUT

Look to see the triggers at work. Once you identify them, you can start planning on what action you can take.

The workload could be a significant problem; maybe if you started to delegate areas of your work that are not a priority, it would give you space in your head to concentrate on the hectic deadlines you have looming.

Start rationally evaluating your job. Ask yourself what has changed over the past few years that has left you disillusioned and disappointed.

Ask yourself, has the organisation changed its vision or have you changed and you are no longer interested in this type of work.

Sometimes, you have to admit that it's time for something fresh and different.

CHAPTER 7.6 WHAT YOU NEED TO KNOW TO START THE RECOVERY FROM GUILT, SHAME, AND REGRET.

We can't change our past, but we can take steps to make sure it doesn't contaminate our future.

The following are steps to help us let go of regrets.

1. Accept we all make mistakes. If we prolong the regret, it will start to affect our well-being and our health.

2. Stop listening to critical internal dialogue by challenging your thinking.

You will then be able to replace them with a more definite statement.

3. Practice deep breathing and self-care.

4. Focus on gratitude.

Shame and guilt are easily confused. Shame says there is something wrong with who I am, but on the other hand, guilt says there is something wrong in what I am doing or what I have done.

Guilt is also just not about what others are saying about you, it's what you are saying to yourself. It's a form of condemnation. When you are feeling shame, you will resist self-forgiveness. Stuck in toxic shame patterns are common.

The first step is to stop being so hard on yourself. It's easy to fall into a pattern of self-criticism which is emotionally draining.

Unfortunately, shame corrodes the part of us that believes we can't change.

So if you try to shame someone into changing, it won't work as you are only reinforcing them to be worthless and unimportant.

Take, for instance, a child who wets the bed, and then the parent humiliates the child by broadcasting to the rest of the family. The parent may think they are teaching the child to be more grown-up and not to be such a baby. Not so, all they are doing is shaming the child. By adopting this strategy, it will only prolong the bedwetting habit for the child.

The following are techniques to help let go of guilt and shame:

1. Even if you feel you have done something to feel guilty, forgive yourself; no one is perfect.

2. Ask yourself what have I learned from the experience.

3. Look at what makes you proud. Immerse yourself in all the positive aspects of your life. Overwhelm your mind with all the good stuff.

4. Because guilt says, there is something wrong in what I have done, sometimes to make amends you may need to ask someone for forgiveness. By doing this, it will help release you from negative thoughts.

5. Recognise that when you are experiencing shame, it's easy to act out and make the situation worse.

E.g., You are in a crowded room; you feel belittled after someone disrespectfully spoke to you. Because you are ashamed of how it made you feel, you retaliate and shout back. Unfortunately, this reinforces the feelings of shame.

6. As regards to sexual abuse, even if it happened years ago, tell a trusted person. The best cure for shame is to talk about it. Carrying this burden of shame is not yours to carry; it solely belongs to the predator. Talk about your feelings. Share the secret. Don't hide it. Find a professional counsellor to help you get an understanding of the trauma. Even join a support group, this will all help to lift the load from your

shoulders. By starting to adopt these new behaviours, a pathway of recovery will soon begin. The burden of shame will become lighter.

CHAPTER 7.7 MAKE YOUR ANGER WORK FOR YOU.

Anger is a normal emotion. It only gives us a problem when it's not managed correctly. When a person gets angry for whatever reason, the initial goal is to:

1. Cap escalation of the anger. You don't want to do anything that would ignite the anger any more. At this stage, it's best to separate yourself from the event or person that has triggered the anger.

2. Identify your anger. If you feel justified by the anger, allow yourself to own it. Allow yourself to say, 'Yes, I'm justified to be angry, for what that person did.'

3. Change your focus; instead of saying to yourself, 'How can that person do this to me?' say 'I wonder what makes that person lose their temper so easily.'

'Why is that person so unhappy?' By doing this, you are coming from a state of anger to curiosity and hopefully, on to compassion.

By doing this, you may be more open to seeing the other person's point of view. All their life, they could have been abused, betrayed, and treated poorly. Along comes yourself, and the least little thing that happens sends them into a total rage. Continue to keep changing your focus: instead of complaining what has just happened you, look at the blessings of what didn't happen. Staying angry doesn't serve you; however, if you are in a state of gratitude, you will find yourself starting to calm down a lot quicker.

4. It is also helpful at this stage to take deep breaths and allow as much oxygen into your body as possible. If you continue taking shallow breaths, it will take longer for the anger to settle.

Finally, remember if a situation triggers you into a rage, you are giving your power away. No one wants to answer to the consequences of anger/rage. However, by losing control, that's what you are doing. You are giving away control. Worst-case scenario, because of anger, you'll let a judge decide how many years jail you have to serve because of your actions. If that happens, you will end up with no choices or power.

CHAPTER 7.8 ALLOW YOURSELF COMPASSION AND BECOME YOUR OWN BEST FRIEND

The key to self-compassion is to always look beyond your pain and suffering. Look past your shame; look to who you were created to be. Part one of this book shows how easy it is to be weighed down with anger, unforgiveness, etc. from our past. So many people stay broken because of the mistakes they have made. The power of the Gospel gives you a fresh new heart; it doesn't matter what you have done. God doesn't see you for what you have done, but he sees what you can become. Broken, abused people find it hard to let go of the hurt and betrayals that happened to them. However, in Psalm 42, the psalmist shifts the focus on himself.

Why are you cast down, O my soul?
And why are you disquieted within me?
Hope in God, for I shall yet praise Him
For the help of His countenance. Psalm 42.5

He sees himself through the eyes of God. Challenge your feelings of not being good enough. Don't listen to the voice of criticism. Go against your feelings. Sometimes the best thing you can do in dealing with hurt and depression – is to take your eyes off it. Fix your eye on who you are. See the way God sees you. You don't need to live your life carrying unwanted baggage from your past. In other words, don't let your past define your story.

Start showing self-compassion, love God as yourself. When we try to love people and hate ourselves, it doesn't work as you will feel worthless. Keep reminding yourself how God sees you and how precious you are.

Permit yourself to be your own best friend. When you're compassionate and supportive of yourself, your fears and criticism will go down. By letting go of the baggage that you have been carrying for years, it will create new headspace. By doing this, it will also help you to accomplish more and have access to greater creativity.

CHAPTER 7.9 HOW TO STOP SABOTAGING YOU LIFE - TIPS ON HOW TO STOP SELF-HARMING AND HOW TO LET GO OF LIMITING BELIEFS

TIPS ON HOW TO STOP SELF-HARMING

As spoken in Chapter 6.8, self-harming is all about control. If a person finds it hard to process and deal with mental pain, they think by turning to self-harm they have somehow taken control of the pain. Unfortunately, this is not true, as they have only temporarily masked the emotional pain until it reappears. The following are tips on how to stop self-harming:

1. Keep a note of your triggers. I.e., the area the self-harming takes place; the time it usually happens;

2. Try and reduce the times and places you know when you are at your most vulnerable.

3. Try screaming at the top of your voice. Followed by deep breathing.

4. Do some exercises that leave you out of breath.

5. Wash your face in a basin of cold water.

6. Change your surroundings, if you know your bedroom is the place you usually self-harm. Try and stay out of it as much as possible.

7. Don't be alone, phone a good friend and maybe go to the cinema.

8. Start clearing out cupboards. Set up new projects in the house, you will find it distracting.

9. Wear an elastic band on your wrist. When you feel compelled to self-harm, spring the elastic band against your wrist.

10. Take away all self-harming tools. I.e., razor blades, tissues, and sharp objects from your environment. Don't have any self-harming tools readily available.

11. Write out your feelings. Challenge the negative thinking. Ask where is the evidence to believe what you are thinking?

12. Let go of control - lose the desire to control.

13. Be relaxed about not being in control all the time.

14. Accept, it's okay not to be perfect.

HOW TO HELP PARENTS DEAL WITH THEIR CHILD'S SELF-HARMING BEHAVIOUR

It's not easy for any parent when told their child is self-harming. The child may speak directly to the parent, or the parent may have come across by accident some evidence of the self-harming.

The first step for the parent:

1. LISTEN, DON'T JUDGE – let the child feel you are hearing them. Ask is there anything they need.

2. Ask the child – what they need from you. The child may require you to take them to get urgent medical attention or to get an antibiotic for an infected wound. Or they may need you to hear what they are saying.

3. Arrange a therapist for your child.

4. Don't crowd your child; however, make sure you always check in with them. Reassure them you are still there if they need to talk.

5. Remember, always seek to UNDERSTAND and not JUDGE.

HOW TO LET GO OF LIMITING BELIEFS

Step 1.

The good news is that we can let go of old self-limiting beliefs and develop new, more positive ones. Limiting decisions shape everything you do or not do. The first obstacle is identifying them. Once you do that, you have a choice. You can either continue to believe that belief or replace it with the truth. By recognising how these beliefs manifest themselves in us, we are then in the position of creating a new narrative for ourselves.

Step 2.

Look back into your past and examine the origin of the limiting belief. Relating to my own story, it was when my mother stopped me from sitting the transfer test when I was 11 years of age.

Step 3.

Be honest and fair with yourself. Instead of looking at all the things that went wrong, start looking at the positives. Try concentrating on all the right choices that have contributed to make you the person you are today.

On reflection, I can now see that a lot of children are a lot slower than others in their academical development. I should be thankful to my mother that she had the insight to know that I wasn't ready for a life-changing test at the age of eleven. My passion for academia didn't develop until a lot later in life.

Step 4.

Continue to challenge the limiting beliefs if and when they resurface. Concentrate on the positive outcomes that have come from new affirmed actions. By doing this, it will confirm that the old self-limiting beliefs were false. I am thankful, at the age of eleven, the right decision got made. If I had sat the test and failed, it could have knocked my confidence throughout my childhood. Therefore, I'm glad the way things worked out, or I may not have grown into the person I am today

HOW TO STOP SELF-SABOTAGING

'I have had enough' Jenny sobbed as she walked into my consulting room and flopped down on the seat.

I could see straight away she was not in a great place.

Her hair and clothes looked tossed and unkempt. She explained she had just broken up from her boyfriend and was feeling terrible.

Jenny explained the relationship was significant to her as he was the first person in her life who treated her with love and respect.

Jenny, unfortunately, had a tough life, she was brought up in an abusive home where both parents emotionally and physically abused her.

Over the years, she went from one toxic relationship to another. All that changed when she met her last boyfriend. He seemed to be everything she ever wanted, loyal, loving, and caring.

Jenny explained that it was all her fault they had broken up. She knew herself what she was doing; she would continually start rows with her boyfriend for no reason. Jenny admitted she was only ever content when she brought dissension and drama into the relationship. Eventually, her boyfriend got fed up and advised her to seek professional counselling, as he couldn't continue to handle the display of continued aggression she showed him.

Unfortunately, the above example is a classic example of' Self Sabotage.' You could ask why does someone set out to wreck their own life? Why would anyone take adverse action against themselves?

Sabotage seems illogical on its surface; however, it has its strange logic.
When someone comes from an abusive past, it can sometimes be easier for them to feel disappointment and sadness rather than success and happiness. The person will draw to what their norm was all their life. Therefore, someone coming from a background of abuse will find a relationship that provides contentment and stability very foreign to their psyche

With that said, no wonder Jenny reacted the way she did. All the negative thinking and limiting beliefs of her not being good enough came to the surface when she faced her insecurities.

Like most sabotaging behaviours, they stem from our childhood Because Jenny was brought up in a home where she was made to feel unworthy and unimportant, she then, unfortunately, continued to carry this belief into adult life. If this distorted belief of herself remains unchallenged, she will continue to sabotage and abuse herself with this type of behaviour.

1. Start adapting self-care by making sure you meet your needs. Remember you are important, and you can't make anyone else happy until you are comfortable and at peace with yourself first Find out what it is that you want? Be truthful with yourself! Maybe you are in a relationship and you have lost your identity and don't know who you are anymore. Get to know yourself and start feeling good about who you are and who you want to be.

2. Start challenging negative core beliefs. As in Jenny's case, her core belief formed from her childhood, which made her feel unimportant and unloveable. By testing this particular core belief, she confirmed there was no evidence to say she was unlovable. She had met a good man who loved her. Therefore this core belief is a lie. Jenny can say to herself, 'I am lovable, I am important, and I have the right

to be happy.'

3. Find a professional counsellor to help with self-esteem and confidence issues. Develop self-compassion, and above all, be kind and patient to yourself.

CHAPTER 8.0

- FIND HEALING FROM A CO-DEPENDENCY RELATIONSHIP.

Many people go about their daily life and not be aware that their unconscious belief is to seek approval and validation from everyone. They are so wrapped up in trying to meet the needs of others that they forget about themselves.

- To be healthy and stable, we have to have a healthy internal dialogue.

- So to heal this co-dependency within ourselves, we first have to understand its origin. It could be the fear of not being good enough or feeling of abandonment. Maybe as a child, your mother and father found it difficult to connect with you emotionally. Although they loved and cared for you, they weren't able to validate you for everything you were feeling. Unfortunately, when this happens, a co-dependency develops within us. Our head creates a narrative. 'I have to do this to be loved …'

- Or 'I have to worry about everyone else for them to love and validate me.' In fact, what is happening is that you are continually living in a sense of fear; a core belief has developed, i.e., 'I have to be doing something to seek something.'

- The problem with this is that you are relying on others all the time for approval. To start healing, you have to begin self-soothing.

- Healing starts by not judging yourself on why you were feeling this way. It's beginning to take responsibility for your life. Stop relying on others for validation to make you happy. It doesn't matter if they don't agree with you. Start filling your tank up. Be proud of the person you have become.

The following are tips for co-dependency recovery:

1. Start by knowing what you want. It's okay to feel uncomfortable regardless of the backlash. The people in your life may not like your new boundaries. You will receive criticism for acting selfishly. People may put you on a guilt trip.

2. Let go of the need to fix others. You don't have to rescue; they are on their own journey. They have to fix themselves.

3. Be more self-aware; realise that it wasn't your problem in the first place.

4. Past relationships that were toxic start to shift, some will leave for good. Restoration with friends and family will take place. Mutual respect will be the basis of new relationships.

5. The new relationships will be stable and have healthy boundaries. They will be not too open or too rigid.

All of the above steps are a great way forward to help in the healing of a co-dependent relationship. Given this, it's always a good idea to seek a counsellor who can serve as an unbiased third party.

Remember if your relationship is worth saving, it's worth putting the extra work into it. The ultimate goal of forming a healthy relationship is that both people have fully formed identities outside their time together. So when they come together, they create a relationship that allows them to be themselves.

HELP! MY PARTNER SAYS I'M A CONTROL FREAK

Hopefully, this book outlines the negative impact of carrying chronic control issues around with you. It shows how detrimental these behaviours are, especially if you are the one who is the catalyst of the control. The following steps will help you stand back a bit and start being more self-aware.

a. Don't confuse imagination with reality, just because your partner has a different opinion than you, doesn't mean that they don't care for you. Respect their opinion and choice. Learn to let your partner breath and be themselves in the relationship.

b. Don't punish your present boyfriend for the betrayals of an ex. Once you ask your boyfriend a question, don't hound him if he has never given you any reason to distrust him. Accept his word. Let go of the past hurts. Don't allow old memories of days gone by to contaminate the present as well as your future.

c. Don't snoop, once you start doing this sort of habit, it won't stop. The last thing you want is your boyfriend to catch you. Always work towards open and honest communication with each other.

d. Accept that your partner has outside responsibilities and interests apart from you. Children from a previous relationship will still need their dad and mom. Never try to control when your partner is to see his children. If there is a conflict of interests, always try to reach a compromise through mutual discussion.

e. If your partner has a particular bad dress sense, there is no harm in encouraging them to dress more appropriately. However, always remember your partner is a person in their own right. They have their own character and personality. By allowing them to be that person, will give them the freedom of being themselves within the relationship.

f. Remember trying to control everything will only lead to sorrow. Not just the misery you are giving yourself, but the stress and anxiety you are giving to your partner. Don't look at compromise as losing; look at it as a sign of having understanding and freedom within your relationship.

CHAPTER 8.1 - HOW TO FIND PEACE AND FORGIVE SOMEONE WHO BETRAYED YOU

The theme of this book is all about holding on to stuff you don't need. You may not realise it, but carrying unforgiveness/grudges is like allowing squatters to take up residence in your mind. You don't want them there, they taunt you of past events, and they don't allow you to make room for new experiences.

Forgiveness is defined differently by everyone, but generally, its a decision to let go of a grudge or resentment you're holding against someone. It will give you a sense of peace and will enable you then to move forward.

The act of forgiveness is not an easy road. Like any skill, it has to be put into practice to achieve the benefits.

Begin by allowing yourself to feel the anger. You may have reasonable cause to feel angry, especially if someone betrayed or abused your kindness. You may even think that speaking to the person will help you give closure to this issue. However, it's important if you do talk to the person, you do it positively without accusing or judging. You have a better chance of the other person hearing you if you stay controlled.

If it is not possible to speak to the person concerned, maybe the person has been dead for many years. However, anger and unforgiveness are still there. Try writing a letter to this person, explain how you feel and how they hurt you. You can destroy the letter afterwards if you want.

Sometimes I work this principle in therapy; I may ask a client to imagine the person who hurt them is sitting on the chair next to them. I will then ask the client what would they like to say to this person? By doing this, the client has then been given a safe environment to start to offload and unburden all their negative emotions which they have held for years.

This watershed can be the start of the healing and forgiveness process.

1. Stop trying to tell yourself that everything will be alright if that person could only realise how much they hurt you. The sad truth is, that person may never recognise the hurt they gave you. Don't waste any more of your time waiting for that apology because it may never come. You can still heal and forgive someone without ever getting it. The main thing is that you decide for yourself that you don't want to wake up each day feeling disgruntled and bitter.

Start saying to yourself, "I'm tired of feeling angry with this person. I'm ready to start feeling happy again."

2. Stop blaming every disappointment in life on that particular person. Start taking responsibility for your own decisions and mistakes. Remember, it's not how we started in this life; it's how we will finish, which is important.

3. Deciding to withhold forgiveness can have an adverse opinion of who you are. We may see ourselves as hard and intolerant of others. Learn to be kind to yourself. Start being compassionate to yourself first. By rebuilding the relationship you have with yourself, you will start to see others in a more empathetic mode.

It is important to recognise that forgiveness is not about the other person; it's more about you. It's about allowing yourself to start enjoying the present and looking forward to the future. It's about letting the past stay in the past.

4. Become more self-aware of the impact your behaviour has on others. Instead of being critical and self-righteous, start focusing on why you feel the way you do. Start putting more work into yourself, instead of concentrating on other people's behaviour.

5. When a person's behaviour has hurt you, don't close

down and adopt avoidance behaviour. Choose a good, trusted friend and talk about the impact it has had on you. Failing that, go to see a therapist. The last thing you want to do is bottle it up and let the hurt take root.

6. Remember, you cannot re-write history; what has happened has happened. Unfortunately, bad things befall good people. However, what you can do is start to treasure every moment you have left on this planet. Start appreciating every second. Understandably, you may be angry that someone in your past has caused you great hurt. However, that person has no longer got any control or power in your present or future life – that is unless YOU give him that power.

7. By purging your mind from all the unforgiveness and anger, you will start to feel lighter and more creative. New habits will form, and your subconscious will automatically throw out any distorted thoughts that shouldn't be there.

8. Practice having a thankful heart. Starting adopting new habits that you know will give you a lift at the start of the day, this can range from daily prayer, exercise, or even reading an uplifting book.

9. Recognise the difference between FORGIVENESS and TRUST. You can forgive someone, but it doesn't mean you will instantly trust them. Trust is something earned. The rebuilding of trust will not happen overnight; it will take time. You may also decide not to have this person in your life anymore. That's okay too. Forgiveness is not something you do for the person that wronged you; it's more of a decision that you do for you.

10. Sometimes we have to forgive ourselves first. No one is perfect, as we all make mistakes. Find understanding and awareness of what was happening at the time. Recognise the stress that was taking place.

11. When a significant betrayal or hurt happens, ask yourself what lessons have I learned?

12. Recognise the opportunity you had to grow as a person. When something bad happens, although we may have found it hurtful and uncomfortable, the experience will make us stronger and more confident.

13. Ask yourself, "What was I doing to allow this person to do this to me in the first place?"

"Do I not keep proper boundaries?" "Is there a pattern of abuse taking place?"

14. Forgiveness is not a weakness; it's a sign of courage and strength.

15. Try speaking with a therapist or a trusted friend. A therapist will help you to try and get some understanding of the situation. They will even assist you in practising empathy. It is sometimes beneficial to be able to see the viewpoint from the other person's perspective. It can help you to understand their actions and why they did what they did.

16. Remind ourselves, what the benefits of forgiveness are!

- Reduced blood pressure and respiratory levels.

- Feeling lighter and not weighed down

- Feeling motivated and looking forward to an exciting future.

When you feel you don't have the power yourself and feel unable to forgive, remember what Christ did for us on the Cross. Turn to him, and he will lift us up; "I can do all things through Christ who strengthens me

Philippians 4:12-13

One of the significant reasons that keep a person from forgiving is they feel the other person doesn't deserve forgiveness. The person concerned may not care if you forgive them or not. However, what we must remember is, it doesn't matter. What matters is by letting go of the anger and forgiving them, we are setting ourselves free. We are no longer their captive. Nelson Mandella gave a fantastic quote on forgiveness:

- He said, *"Unforgiveness is like drinking poison and hoping it will kill your enemy."*
- By letting go of this enormous burden of unforgiveness, it will set us free. We will feel lighter, and above all, we will have space in our head for new experiences and opportunities.

Bear with each other and forgive whatever grievances you may have against one another. Forgive as the Lord forgave you. Colossians 3:13

CHAPTER 8.2 - IF YOU THOUGHT SETTING BOUNDARIES IN A RELATIONSHIP WERE UNIMPORTANT- READ THIS.

Setting healthy boundaries is an excellent tool for people pleasers. It allows you to have an internal rule book that complies with your own core beliefs and values. Setting healthy boundaries will enable you to make decisions based on what's best for you.

When we first hear the word boundary, we associate it immediately with a physical barrier. For example, the fence surrounding our home separates the land that we own as opposed to the property of our neighbours. A clear boundary like this is very helpful to our everyday life, as it allows us and others to see what areas of land each are responsible for. Example: when it comes to grass cutting. Of course, not all physical boundaries have huge visible fences. Sometimes it just might be some obscure markers that are only known by the relevant owners.

Nonetheless, the vital issue here is that both parties know the boundary exists.

When a physical boundary is breached, it's easy to see and acknowledge the stress it produces. For example, a few weeks ago, my husband and I were both out for the evening. As usual, we secured our home before setting off. We left our two family dogs, one a 6-year-old shitshu and the other a 7-month-old labrador pup lying on their beds in the kitchen. Unfortunately, when we arrived back, we found our house burglarized. Drawers and cupboards containing personal photographs, etc., were pulled out and scattered over the floor. Our first concern was the dogs; thankfully, they were unharmed. However, our house was a bit of a mess. The Police, CID, and forensics visited us for the next few days as we had to give statements and fingerprints. Nothing was stolen; the police said they were looking for cash, anything else didn't interest them.

Once word got out, our family and friends visited and telephoned us. They asked how we were coping as they understand the stress and anxiety a burglary/home invasion can cause.

This Home invasion experience highlighted to me how easy it was for others to sympathize and understand if the boundary violation is physical and easily seen. Unfortunately, this is not always the case. As previously discussed in this chapter, the majority of stress and anxiety experienced by people are related to an implicit boundary violation. In other words, when relational and emotional boundaries are violated, the impact of this trauma is not apparent to others.

Of course, we can't set up fences or door locks to protect ourselves from relational stress. However, we can set up a series of guidelines and rules that help us to stay focused on our own set of values

By knowing what your values are, you can then set up systems that help you to achieve those needs. This process is called 'setting healthy boundaries'.

TIPS ON SETTING HEALTHY BOUNDARIES

- Know what your values are, as it will help you set your boundaries.

- Don't be afraid to tell others of your limitations.

- By respecting your boundaries, you will teach others to respect them too.

- Do not justify or apologize for the boundary you are setting.

- Be respectful, but firm.

- When a boundary violation occurs, communicate it immediately to the other person. If you don't, the healthy protection that you get from the boundary will soon diminish.

Healthy boundaries are a crucial factor for self-care. Well set up boundaries, help you to be the person you want to be. It will help you find more fulfilment in life and establish your own identity.

Carol was a 35-year-old female teacher. She loved her job teaching English at the local university. When Carol first came to counselling, she presented with panic attacks and anxiety. Carol said she usually had no bother with second-year students; however, this year was different. She felt she hadn't the same control of her students. Carol felt a particular boy would disrespect her in the lecture room. Carol was at the stage where she hated going to work each day.

Carol soon admitted that she had felt sorry for this lad at the beginning of term. He seemed to have a harsh home life, and Carol mistakenly gave him extra attention to help him keep up with his studies. She even accepted him as a friend on Facebook. It wasn't long before Carol realised that the lad was starting to become demanding in class, and she was finding the level of stress hard to handle. Although nothing inappropriate between Carol and the student took place, Carol intended to help the lad. She felt as a student he would have great potential if he got the right encouragement.

Carol and I discussed the reasons why she wanted to help this student. Indeed her motives were honourable and all above board. However, because of the blurring of boundaries, the teacher/student relationship was distorted. She inadvertently gave the student a false perception of her being more of a friend rather than a teacher. This raised the lad's expectation. Unfortunately, when Carol didn't meet the lad's aspiration as a friend, the lad then got nasty and spiteful in the class.

Through the counselling process, Carol realised that on reflection, she gave her student mixed signals, especially agreeing to be his friend on Facebook. Carol learnt the hard way not to mix friend and professional relationships. Thankfully, the lad soon settled down and finished his studies and came out with a 2:1 degree. However, Carol learnt a lesson that boundaries are there not just for your protection; they are also there for the people around you. When others know your limitations and boundaries, they will respect them; however, if you are slack and sluggish, they will be too.

CHAPTER 8.3 - TIPS ON DEALING WITH PASSIVE AGGRESSIVE PEOPLE

If your partner or a member of your family communicates in a passive-aggressive manner, there is no doubt it can be quite challenging for all concerned. It may well be a trait they have always had or a behaviour that just started recently. Either way, it's a clear indication that the person has underlying anger issues about something and is unable to speak directly about it.

To deal with it appropriately, it's first best to examine whether it's a form of mild passive aggression or maybe it's to do with something much more severe.

Dealing with passive aggression that is mild, you can respond to it with silence and say to yourself, 'I don't need to react to this.'

However, how do you handle passive aggression when you know that there is something serious going on, and you feel your boundaries are being breached?
The first step is to make sure you are in a CALM STATE before you communicate with them.

If you know what they want to say, and they won't come out and say it, calmly state what you see. Say the words they are unable to speak.

Be open and genuine. Ask the other person, 'Is something is bothering you, please tell me?'

Remember, you must come from a calm state before opening up this conversation. The last thing you want to be is sarcastic and aggressive yourself.

CHAPTER 8.4 - KNOW HOW TO RECOGNISE PASSIVE AGGRESSIVE LANGUAGE.

The following are examples of passive-aggressive conversation:

'How about we sit in tonight and not go to the party?'
Answer: 'SUIT YOURSELF.'

'I'm sorry it won't happen again.'
Answer: 'IF YOU SAY SO.'

'I would like us to go and see my parents at the weekend.'
Answer: 'FINE.'

CHAPTER 8.5 - HOW TO RECOGNISE TOXIC PEOPLE AND THEN LEARN TO DISARM THEM

It's not easy to recognise toxic people. However, the good news is, you are the gate-keeper of your life! You can let in who you want. You can reclaim your power by not accepting anyone who violates your integrity and values.

However, the bad news is that toxic people are very talented in withholding their true nature. By the time you have discovered their toxicity, it's usually too late, as they have already moved into your life.

When two people start to date at the beginning of their relationship, everything is usually new, exciting, and passionate. They can't get enough of each other as the relationship is in the honeymoon stage. Everyone is on good behaviour.

However, as the relationship starts to develop and the two people start to get to know each other, life events begin to happen in each other's life. Maybe a parent died, or perhaps a person was made redundant. Or maybe one or the other had to endure a significant health scare. There can be any amount of challenges that can affect and pressurise a new and budding relationship.

That's why I always feel it's a good idea for a couple not to rush into the commitment of marriage too soon. There is no more excellent way of getting to know your partner than to see him responding to life's challenges. For example, maybe you went through the sad event of your father's death, and your partner was a great help, he was able to step up and support you at the funeral. You felt content and under no pressure as he stayed in the background and was there for you when you needed him, as he was putting your needs first.

Unfortunately, not all relationships pass through these experiences intact.

The following are behaviours that should be taken seriously, as they can be warning signs that your new partner may be not all he makes out to be:

15 signs you are dealing with a Toxic Person

1. He is exceptionally opinionated and judgemental.

2. Manipulative: would often say, 'If you cared for me you would ...'

3. Chronic sarcasm, always trying to put someone down.

4. Has a controlling nature: 'I don't think you suit that dress as much as your blue one.'

5. He will be moody and go into a rage quickly. He will use anger to control you.

6. He has extreme insecurities. If you don't agree with him, he will use passive aggression until you reassure him, he is right.

7. Always plays the victim. Has the world view that people are still out to get him.

8. Self-centred, always looking for his needs to be met. What's in it for him.

9. They do their best to avoid responsibility.

10. They never take responsibility for anything they do wrong; it's always someone else's fault.

11. In a relationship, they have all the power and control.

12. You always walk on eggshells around them. Your fear is not to annoy them.

13. You know you are going to suffer if you upset him; this can be done through passive aggression, i.e., silent

treatment for days. Or it could be verbal or physical abuse.

14. Toxic people have no respect for other people's boundaries.

15. Toxic people are usually negative. If they enter a room, the whole atmosphere changes.

There is a significant distinction between a toxic person and someone who is genuinely going through a rough time in their life. A helping hand and a listening ear can be of great benefit to these people.

Some people experience mental health issues. In cases like this, kind words and support are best.

A person who works hard at becoming more self-aware will soon be able to distinguish between the relationships that are healthy and nurturing and the ones that are controlling and toxic.

HOW TO DISARM A TOXIC PERSON

1. When the toxic person critically addresses you, stay calm, take a deep breath, and don't respond immediately.

2. Remember, their one aim is to get a reaction from you.

3. Control your own emotions, stay calm, stay assured, and remember they will only have power if you give it to them.

4. Be prepared to receive some verbal backlash, especially when they realise you have set new boundaries.

5. Instead of falling into their trap of creating more drama - Answer them with the following phrases:-

a. I notice you are upset ...
b. Would you like a glass of water?
c. I hear what you're saying,
d. Let's resume this when you are feeling calmer.

e. I hope you feel better tomorrow.

f. I understand you see it differently from me. However, you have your opinion, and I have mine.

CHAPTER 8.6 - IS IT OKAY TO LET GO OF A TOXIC PERSON?

When Elaine, a 45-year-old secretary, first came to counselling, she was suffering from severe anxiety and panic attacks. Elaine lived with Martin, who was a successful businessman. She met him shortly after her first marriage broke up, and they had been together for the past five years. At first, Elaine thought she hit the jackpot with Martin; he was everything she dreamed of, wealthy, good looking, and charming. However, it wasn't long before Elaine discovered that Martin had many disturbing behaviours. Martin, had a nasty temper as he would continually fly off into a rage if he didn't get what he wanted. Elaine had tried to leave him for years but always hoped he would change. However, it got to the point that she couldn't take any more. Her two adult children never saw much of Elaine; in fact, they hadn't seen their mother for six months. Martin didn't care much for them; he made it clear he didn't want them to visit. Elaine didn't see much of any of her family.

Elaine knew if she walked away from the relationship, it would be a struggle financially, as she didn't earn that much as a secretary.

However, Elaine got to the stage she couldn't live with the emotional and verbal abuse any longer. During our counselling sessions, Elaine admitted that she was scared to walk away, in case she would regret it. She didn't know what to do for the best.

To help Elaine understand her feelings and fears, I said to her, ask yourself one question, 'What is my cost to stay in this relationship?'

Elaine realised that she was paying a considerable price to stay in the relationship:

a. the cost of not having her family and children in her life, as Martin didn't want them.

b. The cost of not being able to make decisions herself. She always had to get permission from Martin.

c. The cost of not being her true self, as she walked on eggshells, in fear of his anger and upsetting Martin.

Elaine soon came to a firm decision that the cost was too high to stay where she was. She knew it wouldn't financially be easy to go it alone, especially at her age; however, she knew she couldn't afford to stay.

When I next saw Elaine, she was upbeat and relaxed. Once she had decided to leave Martin, she never looked back. She said life had still its challenges, but for the first time in years, she was able to live her life and be her true authentic self. She was just back from a girly weekend with her two daughters. Life, at last, was looking up for her.

Just like the analogy of the train, people will walk in and walk out of our lives. When people get off the train, it can hurt at the beginning. However, we know in our hearts that it's for the best. The secret is to stay on the train. Stay on track, and who knows who will get on at the next station.

CHAPTER 8.7 - HOW TO TRANSFORM A GOOD RELATIONSHIP WITH YOUR PARTNER, INTO AN AMAZING ONE

As Alana walked Into my consulting room, she pointed to her phone, and sheepishly sighed, 'That's so typical of him.' My husband hasn't spoken directly to me for a week, however now that he wants something, he sends me a text.

Alana knew her marriage wasn't right. She and her husband rarely sat down to have a conversation these days. In fact, Alana openly admitted if they did sit down to talk, it usually turned into a full-blown row. That's probably one of the reasons why they communicated a lot through text.

Initially, Alana had come to counselling for help with her anxiety. It transpired that she still loved her husband, and she believed he always loved her. However, over time, she felt, each of them was drifting further apart.

A healthy relationship has to be worked at. It's not easy sometimes. However, the payoff is amazing when two people can connect.

The top tips for improving communication are:-

1. Sit down and talk with each other. Take time to be alone and really listen to the other person. Let them say what they have to. Speak when they have finished talking; it's so important not to interrupt. Ask friendly and appropriate questions. Don't overwhelm each other with too much too soon. Take a step at a time. Be generous in sharing.

2. Be prepared to compromise. Most people are scared to make changes. They like to keep people and situations the same. People are afraid of change as they are not ready for it. When a relationship is healthy, change and growth are allowed to develop.

3. Self-care. People forget that to make other people happy, they first have to feel satisfied themselves. Therefore self-

care is so important, Before trying to meet other people's needs, make sure your own basic needs are met first. A good healthy relationship is mutual, it's meant that the two people are happy, not just one.

4. Be there for each other and be each other's rock. In other words, make the relationship trustworthy.

5. Don't set unrealistic expectations. Try and avoid constant disappointments by always expecting too much. Start to see things as they actually are and not base them on how you would like them to be.

6. Show emotional warmth. Don't be afraid to show kindness to your partner. Sometimes a big hug to your partner can be better than a multitude of words.

7. The best relationships are ones that you can be yourself. If you try and pretend you're something you're not, it usually catches up with you. Healthy relationships are made of real people. Remember, none of us is perfect.

CONCLUSION

Let's step back and review the ethos of this book. First and foremost, it concerns the mental baggage we are carrying around. The main contributors of this baggage are negative emotions, stemming from old unresolved anger, guilt, shame, and unforgiveness. Unfortunately, this baggage in caustic and affects our mental health.

Part two of the book outlines the unhealthy addictive behaviours we adopt to cope with the complexities of these negative emotions. Unfortunately, these addictive behaviours end up more damaging than the original problem.

The book highlights the impact that emotional baggage has on our lives. It shows that most people are unaware of how destructive and loaded they are. It can range from 'People-Pleasing', 'Passive-aggressiveness', 'Obsessive control issues', and 'Choosing the wrong partners', to name but a few. This book highlights the importance of why 'Travelling Light' is paramount to our mental health.

Part three of the book outlines the tools and techniques we can adopt to replace these unhealthy habits. Hopefully, this will also help us to become more self-aware and allows us to be the best possible version of ourselves.

The aim is not to waste our precious moments on Earth. The time that God has allotted to us on this journey will be over before we know it. We want to make the most of every second he has given us. To do this, we first have to start by examining our lives and let go of the emotional debris that holds us back.

By reading this book, it will hopefully be the turning point of a fantastic transformation of your life.

If you feel you would benefit from any extra support to help with this process, I would also urge you to make an appointment with a professionally trained counsellor.

In conclusion, I would now refer back to the train metaphor first discussed in the Introduction of this book.

Of course, pleasant memories will happen on our train journey. However, there will be times when the train will pass through difficult and dark tunnels, such as:
- the death of a loved one
- having a major illness
- divorce or separation
- loss of a job.

God doesn't want us to make the wrong choices in life, but because we have free will, we sometimes choose to get off at the wrong stop. However, as long as we turn around and get back on track, the dark tunnel will eventually come to an end. By remembering to keep God as our 'Engine master', we will safely reach our destination.

REFERENCES

CHAPTER 1

Vicki Norris – Pruning Principle: (Restoring order)
https://restoringorder.com/organizing-is-like-weeding/

CHAPTER 1

Core beliefs are basic beliefs about ourselves, other people, and the world we live in. They are things we hold to be absolute truths deep down, underneath all our "surface" thoughts. Essentially, core beliefs determine how you perceive and interpret the world.
https://www.betterrelationships.org.au/well-being/core-beliefs-self-acceptance/

CHAPTER 3

- Passive-aggressive behaviour is characterized by a pattern of indirect resistance to the demands or requests of others and an avoidance of direct confrontation.[1] Pretending not to understand is a typical passive
https://en.wikipedia.org/wiki/Passive-aggressive_behavior

CHAPTER 5

FEAR - Fear is a feeling induced by perceived danger or threat that occurs in certain types of organisms, which causes a change in metabolic and organ functions and ultimately a change in behavior, such as fleeing, hiding, or freezing from perceived traumatic events.
https://en.wikipedia.org/wiki/Fear

CHAPTER 6

INFLUENCING WELLBEING: MATERIALISM AND SELF-ESTEEM
https://www.psychologytoday.com/gb/blog/in-the-

neighborhood/201403/influencing-wellbeing-materialism-and-self-esteem

CHAPTER 6.1

BURNOUT – Herbert Freudenbergen (1974) - https://www.ncbi.nlm.nih.gov/pubmed/29119764

CHAPTER 6.8

SELF-HARMING – https://www.nhs.uk/news/mental-health/nearly-quarter-14-year-old-girls-uk-self-harming-charity-reports/

CHAPTER 6.8

ATTACHMENT STYLE - https://www.verywellmind.com/john-bowlby-biography-1907-1990-2795514

CHAPTER 6.9

CO-DEPENDENCY - is a behavioural condition in a relationship where one person enables another person's addiction, poor mental health, immaturity, irresponsibility, or under-achievement.[1
https://en.wikipedia.org/wiki/Codependency

THE HOLY BIBLE – New International Version HODDER AND STOUGHTON (LONDON)

Printed in Great Britain
by Amazon